CHRISTIAN ZIONISM 101

I0115947

10 REASONS CHRISTIANS SHOULD SUPPORT ISRAEL *and the* JEWISH PEOPLE

ALBERT JACKSON McCARN

ENDORSEMENTS

By sheer numbers, most Zionists would consider themselves Evangelicals. But would most Evangelicals consider themselves Zionists? Probably not, because Zionism is neither defined nor commonly taught from the pulpit. We Evangelicals should read this book. We should hear the case made for Zionism herein, and decide whether we are Zionists or not.

For those who already accept the Zionist label, Al's book reveals Zionism as something more. It invites followers of Jesus to enter into the narrative which will culminate world history. It invites us to dip our cup into a well of Jesus' love for His people. It invites us to appreciate the fullness of God's greatest-ever social world experiment: bringing forth a people from slavery, asking them to receive upon themselves His own invented culture, and giving them a land in which to live it out. Today God invites the whole world to step into that grand design by accepting that we, through his Son, are spiritually grafted into that same Israel.

Yet, Al's book resists the notion that our Zionism should only be spiritual. He encourages us to connect with the Jewish people now—people like Gidon Ariel whose idea I joined to help him found Root Source. The result is joy. Blaise Pascal said God created a God-shaped vacuum in every human heart that can only be filled by God. I believe He also created a Jewish-shaped vacuum in every Christian that can only be filled by connecting with the Jewish people.

May we all be blessed to self-apply Zionism, to accept our grafted-ness into Israel, and to find the joy of Jewish relationship.

Bob O'Dell, Co-Founder of Root Source and author of *Five Years with Orthodox Jews: How Connecting with God's People Unlocks Understanding of God's Word*

Al McCarn is one of my best friends and a board member of the organization I run, Root Source (www.root-source.com). Now that I have gotten that full disclosure out of the way, I can tell you that I have never seen such a concise and comprehensive book about Christian Zionism, explaining its origins and history, why it is imperative, and bringing a beginner up to expert level in less than 200 pages. Whether your heart already yearns for what God is doing for and with the Jewish People and Israel, or if you are perplexed by it all, this book will help you look through the glass clearly.

Gidon Ariel, CEO and Co-Founder of Root Source in Hebron, Israel

As I read this book, I felt tears prick my eyes and shivers ran down my spine. The Holy Spirit moved within me. The truth within these pages needs to be shouted from pulpits across the globe. These words will light up the dark places within the psyche of the church still blinded by those ancient, intrenched scales. A must-read for those ready for the next phase in world history.

S.J. Ratcliffe, author of *Stones of Wrath: The Tapestry and Stones of Wrath: The Twins*

Christian Zionism 101 is a timely and essential guide to understanding the spiritual bond between Christians and Jews and the calling for Christians to stand with Israel. After witnessing the horrific October 7th terrorist attack and the alarming rise of antisemitism in the West that followed, I asked my friend Al McCarn to write this book. Given Al's extensive knowledge and passion for this subject, I was confident he was the perfect person for the task, but the result exceeded even my highest expectations. Informative, accessible, and thought-provoking, *Christian Zionism 101* presents Christians with ten foundational reasons why they should support Israel and the Jewish people. It is a must-read for anyone seeking clarity on this critical issue.

David Wilber, author of *How Jesus Fulfilled the Law* and *Remember the Sabbath*.

I enthusiastically recommend Albert McCarn's profound exploration of Israel's biblical and historical significance. This work is a meticulously researched and spiritually insightful examination of the land of Israel, its historical context, and its profound theological importance for Jews and Christians.

McCarn's text demonstrates remarkable historical accuracy and biblical integrity. He carefully traces the biblical narrative from Abraham's time through modern history, providing readers with a comprehensive understanding of the land's significance. Albert's approach is both scholarly and deeply respectful, drawing directly from biblical texts and historical documentation to illuminate the ongoing importance of Israel.

What sets this work apart is its critical message for Christians today: understanding Israel is not just a historical exercise but a fundamental aspect of the Christian faith. McCarn compellingly argues that the land of Israel is not merely a geographical location but a central component of God's redemptive plan. He emphasizes that Christians cannot fully comprehend their faith without understanding Israel's biblical and contemporary significance.

McCarn's writing is critical in today's global context, where misinformation and political rhetoric often obscure the deep historical and spiritual roots of the Jewish people's connection to their homeland. He meticulously documents land purchases, historical events, and biblical promises, demonstrating the Jewish people's long-standing connection to the land.

Perhaps most importantly, the book calls Christians to a deeper understanding of their faith's roots. It challenges readers to move beyond superficial interpretations and engage with the profound theological significance of Israel in God's redemptive plan. I recommend this book without reservation to Christians seeking to deepen their understanding of biblical history, those interested in the Middle East's complex history, and anyone wanting to gain a more nuanced perspective on the significance of Israel.

David E. Jones, PhD, Senior Pastor of *Ruach Ministries International*

Al McCarn, in *Christian Zionism 101* lays the much-needed foundational understanding of Zionism and the many reasons why Christians should support Israel and the Jewish people. Beginning with our Lord and savior which is our Jewish Messiah, the blessings Christians receive by blessing Israel and the Jewish chosen people and their land which was an eternal promised covenant land unlike any other. That as Christians through the blood of Yeshua/Jesus that was shed at calvary we have entered into the same spirit of adoption into the Commonwealth of Israel as living stones in the Temple of the God of Israel. As Al so eloquently leads us into a greater understanding of our role in the final unity of Jesus' prayer of unity found in John 17 we also see our part in the ministry of reconciliation of His Body, both Jew and Gentile abiding together as two branches in the root of Yeshua, the Olive Tree. We can now plainly see with eyes of spiritual understanding the final restoration of all things mentioned in Joel as we move in these end days back to the restitution of all things as they were meant in their original intent. These 5 main restorative phases have taken place, first, beginning in 1948 as Israel was born in a day, then secondly in 1967 when Jerusalem was reunited, thirdly, through many decades of Aliyah thousands of Jewish people returned from all over the world as the nations gathered home again, fourthly, the entire world has watched as the actual land became fruitful again just as the ancient prophetic scriptures said they would, and the final fifth phase is the church returning to its Hebraic roots in Yeshua.

Kevin Jessip, President of Global Strategic Alliance

My friend Al McCarn is a Christian and I am an Orthodox Jew living in the Land of Israel. We disagree on a number of important theological issues. Nevertheless, his new book *Christian Zionism 101* points to a shift through which we are all, Jews and Christians, living. I originally coined the term "Torah awakening among non-Jews" when I started to meet Christians like McCarn who came to understand that the Torah, long thought of as belonging exclusively to the Jews, is relevant to their spiritual journeys as well.

Speaking to Christian readers, McCarn explains why Christians who do not yet identify as Christian Zionists should study the historical and biblical record and reconsider their position. Urging more Christians to align with Israel and to identify as Christian Zionists is certainly a move in the right direction, as the world gets ever closer to Redemption.

As an Orthodox Jew encouraging Christians to read this book, I am explicitly not endorsing Christian theology that conflicts with Torah. I am, however, acknowledging that anyone who reveres Hebrew scripture cannot help but conclude that God is a Zionist. And as McCarn challenges his Christian readers, "If God is a Zionist, shouldn't we also be Zionists?"

Rivkah Lambert Adler, PhD, Editor of *Ten From the Nations: Torah Awakening Among Non-Jews*

Al has done a fantastic job answering the "why" concerning Israel. He details the good news of Israel's restoration and what it means for Christians to stand on the Promises of The God of Abraham, Isaac, and Jacob. He also dives into the prophetic consequences of not standing. Every pastor, teacher, and layperson must abandon their replacement mindset and embrace the touchable reality of Biblical Prophecy in this generation.

Tommy Waller, Founder and President of *HaYovel*

To My Nephew John:

Godly young people like you are the inspiration for this book.
This is my best effort at answering your question about why Israel is
important.

CONTENTS

LIST OF MAPS

ACKNOWLEDGMENTS

I offer my profound thanks to everyone who has helped me on this journey, beginning with the God of Abraham, Isaac, and Jacob. Jesus of Nazareth, my Rabbi, has guided me on this journey since I was a child, and I am confident he will guide me to the ultimate destination.

My wife, Charlayne, has been my companion, chief editor, and voice of reason for nearly 40 years. I could not have asked for a better person to fill those roles.

David Wilber, my good friend and publisher, asked me to write this book. He is one of the finest biblical scholars I know, and it is an honor to collaborate with him.

If you find this book easy to read and useful, you can join me in thanking my friends who have had a hand in editing the manuscript. Greg and Anisa Larramore were the first to volunteer. David Altman and Dr. David E. Jones have provided continuous encouragement and kept me on track. The same is true of Bob O'Dell, and my colleagues Steve Wearp and Russ Smith from Ten From the Nations. One good turn deserves another, and that's why I am glad Susanne Ratcliffe took a look at the manuscript. Her novels about Israel's Lost Tribes are another part of this expanding story, and her expedition into the world of authorship continues to inspire me.

This book owes much to the contributions of many, even if they don't yet realize it. Among them are Jeff and Robin Apthorp, Jeff and Vicki Arioli, Dan and Kristi Bush, Aviyah Chaverim, Angie Clark, Rick and Ronna Lee Corriveau, Zach and Julia Jarvis, Tim and Amy Knighten, Jonathan and Hannah Mayhorn, Albert and Tiffany Pennachio, Jason, Katie, Riley, and Kallie Price, Dan Robinson, Jacob and Julia

Salvo, Matthew and Jenny Vander Els, Pete and Ashleigh Wilson, Ethan Winfrey, and all my friends at Founded in Truth Fellowship. You are my extended family in faith. To Shannon-Rachael and Jordan Pulley, Kathryn and Ben Cohen, and Caleb and Megan Cohen, you are not only part of my spiritual family, but my actual family. Thank you for the countless conversations over the years (even those where we agreed to disagree). That's what iron sharpening iron is all about.

My friends at B'ney Yosef North America have been instrumental in helping shape the ideas of this book. Michail and Melanie Bantseev, Ed and Wendy Boring, John and Joie Conrad, David and Faith Jones, Barry and Laura Phillips, Mark and Pollyanna Webb, and Suuqiina and Qaumaniq are my elders. Their counsel is invaluable, as is the counsel of Frank Houtz and Dan and Kathy Collier, my elders of blessed memory. Ephraim and Rimona Frank and Mikell Clayton are among my elders as well, although they have not officially carried that title. Also invaluable is the counsel and friendship of Marcus Bowman, Julia Johnson, Ron and Candi Runyon, Solomon Lopez, Scott Nickerson, Tzefania Pappas, Greg Raley, and Mark Randall.

I am indebted to my Jewish friends and colleagues in Israel and America. Without your friendship and counsel I could not have come to understand the beauty of Israel and the Jewish people, and your living connection to the God of the Universe. To Rabbi Elan and Dr. Rivkah Lambert Adler, Gidon and Devra Ariel, Adam Eliyahu Berkowitz, Rabbi Jonathan Feldstein, David Nekrutman, Ilan Pomeranc, Hanoch Young, Michael Stolz, and Rabbi Tuly Weisz, *toda raba*.

Those who have worked tirelessly in Christian-Jewish relations and in intercession for Israel have been my inspiration for many years. They include Tommy and Sheri Waller and their family, Steve and Doris Wearp and their family, Dean Bye, Tim Heikoop, Jocelyn Parent, Hadassah Mathenge, and Chaim Malespin.

Special thanks to J. Thomas Smith, Lt. Col. (Ret) Glenn Wright, and Dai Sup Han, my colleagues and brothers at Prayer Surge Now.

The prayers of many faithful intercessors have made this work possible and have encouraged me over the years. I am particularly grateful to Audrey Clements, Beverly Hall, Bev Dennen, Laura Densmore, Donna Matts, Barbara Wilkins, and Sister Georjean Allenbach.

Chris Mitchell and Kevin Jessip have labored long to see Jerusalem become the praise in the earth that God has promised it would be. Thank you for your vision. It is an honor to call you brothers in this heavenly calling.

Finally, a very special thanks to Ella Corriveau. The audience I most desire to reach are young people like you. It is you who will carry this restoration process forward, and that is why I value input from a young person who loves the Lord, loves his word, and loves his people. Thanks for accepting that role. May your voice be filled with the messages from our God's heart that will bring multitudes into his Kingdom.

THE ETERNAL BOND OF CHRISTIAN ZIONISM

Shortly after October 7th, 2023, Israel's Government Press Office offered journalists the opportunity to see raw footage from that horrific day. For more than forty minutes, I along with other reporters witnessed some of the most barbaric acts caught on camera, much of it filmed by the Hamas terrorists themselves. We saw terrified children, families, and young adults experiencing unspeakable horrors. When driving back to Jerusalem that day, the words came to my heart, "Honor them." Honor those men, women, and children who weren't just killed that day but mutilated, humiliated, and desecrated. October 7th stands as the worst day in the history of the Jewish people since the Holocaust.

But then within days, antisemitism exploded around the world. From the streets of New York City, Sydney, Amsterdam, and dozens of other cities, anti-Semitic mobs gathered, chanting slogans such as, "From the river to the sea, Palestine will be free!" Even though the people of dozens of kibbutzim next to the Gaza Strip were attacked, suddenly these crowds blamed Israel and demonized the Jewish people. The following spring, college campuses like Columbia University became battlegrounds where highly organized and well-funded activists threatened, assaulted, and intimidated Jewish students. Social media amplified those voices of Jewish hate with millions of text messages and memes. Much like 9-11, October 7th represents the end of one era and the beginning of another. Suddenly, we witnessed a watershed in human history and a demarcation where good was called evil and evil was called good. It's in this new world where Christians are confronted with a choice and the need to decide, "Where do we stand?" Why support Israel and the Jewish people "for such a time as this"? Some believe the church finds itself in a "Dietrich Bonhoffer moment" that refers to the courageous German pastor who dared to stand against the vitriol of the Nazi ideology sweeping pre-WWII Germany.

Al McCarn's *Christian Zionism 101: Ten Reasons Christians Should Support Israel and the Jewish People* provides a compelling and straightforward answer to these questions. In this powerful primer, McCarn clearly lays out the Biblical, historical, and moral reasons why supporting Israel and the Jewish people is a non-negotiable for Bible-believing Christians. *Christian Zionism 101* gives a rock-solid framework from the pages of history and scripture as to why standing with Israel and the Jewish people is not just an option but a necessity for the days we live in. The people of Israel and Jews worldwide need that support now.

Christian Zionism 101 recognizes the prophetic role Christians play in these last days and presents the Biblical truths that God has called a special people whose promises are eternal and unchanging. It acknowledges Israel's unique role in the unfolding story of God's redemptive plan and embraces the Biblical mandate to stand with the Jewish people as stewards of God's covenant. This book offers a roadmap for understanding how this movement fosters hope, deepens faith, and strengthens the unbreakable bond between Christians, Israel, and the Jewish people.

Christian Zionism is more than a theological stance—it's a profound expression of faith, rooted in the Bible's promises and God's enduring covenant with the Jewish people. *Christian Zionism 101: Ten Reasons Why Christians Should Support Israel and the Jewish People* offers a concise yet compelling case for why believers must embrace this truth. This book equips readers with scriptural insights, historical context, and practical applications for supporting Israel. It's a timely guide for Christians eager to align their hearts with God's purposes and play a vital role in His unfolding plan.

Through these pages, may you gain a renewed appreciation for the significance of Israel and the importance of standing with her in prayer and steadfast support. Discover how this shared story is not just history, but a living testament to the faithfulness of God and His purpose for the nations.

Chris Mitchell
Middle East Bureau Chief
CBN News
Jerusalem, Israel

PREFACE

This book is evidence that love truly does cover all offenses. That, I believe, is one of the greatest lessons our God wants us to learn. Can we find common ground with others who have good reason not to trust us, and with whom we disagree? Every time we do that, we take a step closer to the final redemption of the world.

The people who have contributed to this project have many valid reasons to disagree. They include Evangelical Christians, Messianic believers, Orthodox Jews, and people of many other backgrounds who probably never will know how their life work has influenced me.

It is no secret that Jews and Christians have profound disagreements in how they interpret the body of scripture they both consider authoritative. Even within Judaism and Christianity, disagreements over doctrine and application of scripture continue to divide us into sects, causing us to exclude one another from fellowship and attack one another for real or perceived faults. That is true as well for Messianic believers (Jewish and non-Jewish) and Pronomian Christians who find themselves in that liminal space where Judaism and Christianity intersect.

Solomon teaches us that there is nothing new under the sun. That means the divisions of those who profess to be God's people by virtue of their connection to the faith of Abraham have been with us for a long time. The New Testament gives us a picture of how those divisions impacted the people of God two thousand years ago. That is the story of the book of Acts. It is my belief that we will have to revisit every issue covered in Acts before the advent of Messiah's Kingdom. Hopefully we will come to a better outcome than the emerging church and the

Pharisees, Sadducees, Herodians, Essenes, and Zealots attained in the generations following the careers of Jesus and his apostles.

That is the intent of *Christian Zionism 101*. I cannot solve or even address all the issues that divide us, but I can emphasize the common ground we share. That common ground should enable us to move forward together. As my friend David Nekrutman says, Christians and Jews are in a covenantal relationship. He speaks of this as a mystery, and I agree. I believe it is the same mystery Paul writes about when addressing Gentile followers of Jesus and Jews who may or may not have agreed with them about Jesus' messianic claims. The fact is, we are all called into the same Messianic Kingdom, and that Kingdom is the eternal Covenant Commonwealth of Israel. What is indisputable is that the Jewish people are the direct descendants of Abraham, Isaac, and Jacob, the Patriarchs of that Covenant Nation. All the rest of us who cannot prove our lineage have nevertheless pledged allegiance to the God of Israel, seeing that salvation and redemption comes through no other God and no other Covenant.

In that sense, we are the spiritual descendants of the mixed multitude who followed Moses out of Egypt; of Rahab the Canaanite; Ruth the Moabitess; Uriah the Hittite; Ittai the Gittite; Cornelius the Roman Centurion; and Luke the Greek physician. All of them realized in some way the truth that Jesus spoke to the Samaritan woman at the well: salvation is from the Jews (John 4:22). That is why we Christian Zionists follow in the footsteps of these ancestors in seeking good for the Jewish people and nation, knowing that our final redemption is bound up with theirs.

To be honest, it takes a lot of faith for Christians to cultivate relationships based on love and mutual respect with Jews who do not share our devotion to Jesus, the one we believe is the divine Messiah of Israel. In the same way, it takes great faith and tolerance for my Orthodox Jewish friends to reciprocate these relationships, knowing that we identify with Jesus, and that we might at any moment seek to convert them to our way of thinking.

In ages past, and even in our present time, the evangelical nature of Christianity has been an existential threat to Jews and Judaism. That is changing, thanks largely to the existence of the Jewish State of Israel. As one of my Jewish friends says, he is not worried about Christian prose-lytizing or missionary efforts because as a Jew living in Eretz Israel (the Land of Israel) he is simply not in danger of converting.

Maybe this is the prescription for us all: security in our identity. I am secure in my identity with Christ. After half a century of relationship with him, I am not in danger of denying Jesus and converting to any other faith. Why should I expect it to be any different for my Jewish friends who know the Hebrew scriptures better than I ever will, who have a testimony of relationship with the God of Israel, and who live out lives of righteousness that put many Christians to shame?

We're not going to bridge this divide about Jesus, so maybe it's better if we simply acknowledge that we are somehow in covenantal relation-ship with the God of Abraham, Isaac, and Jacob, and by extension with one another. That is my approach to Christian Zionism. I very much want to see all our disagreements resolved, but I know that we can't get there unless we walk this road of faith together.

Albert J. McCarn
December 3, 2024

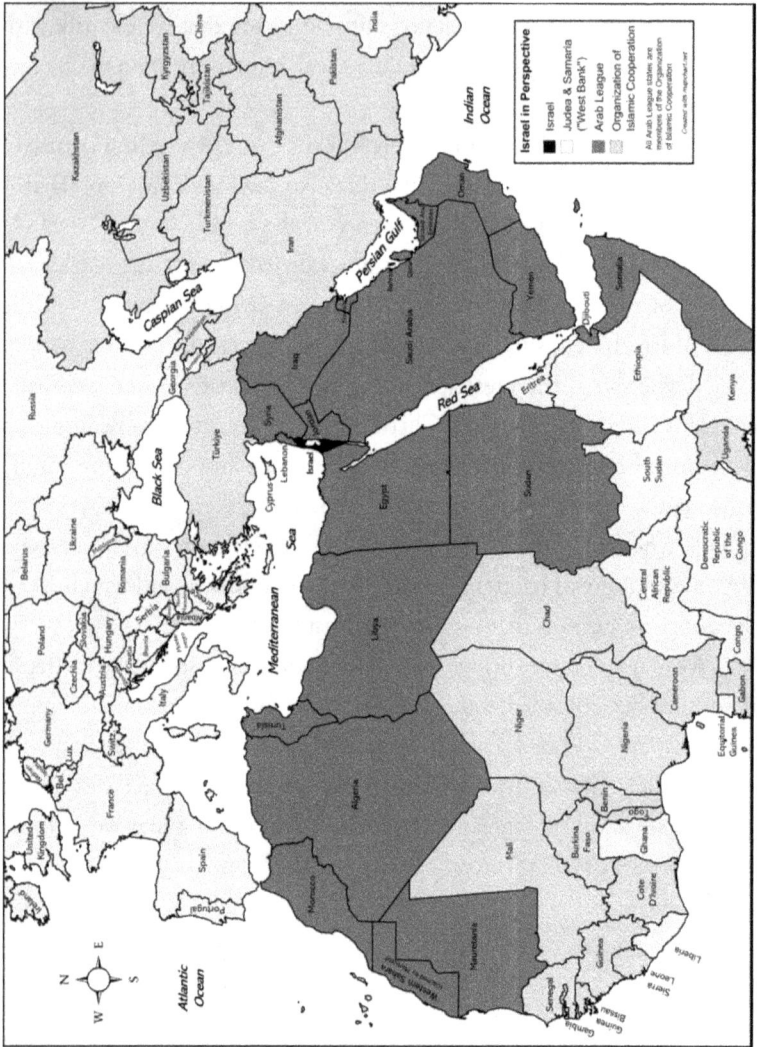

Map 1. Israel in Perspective. (Created with MapChart.)

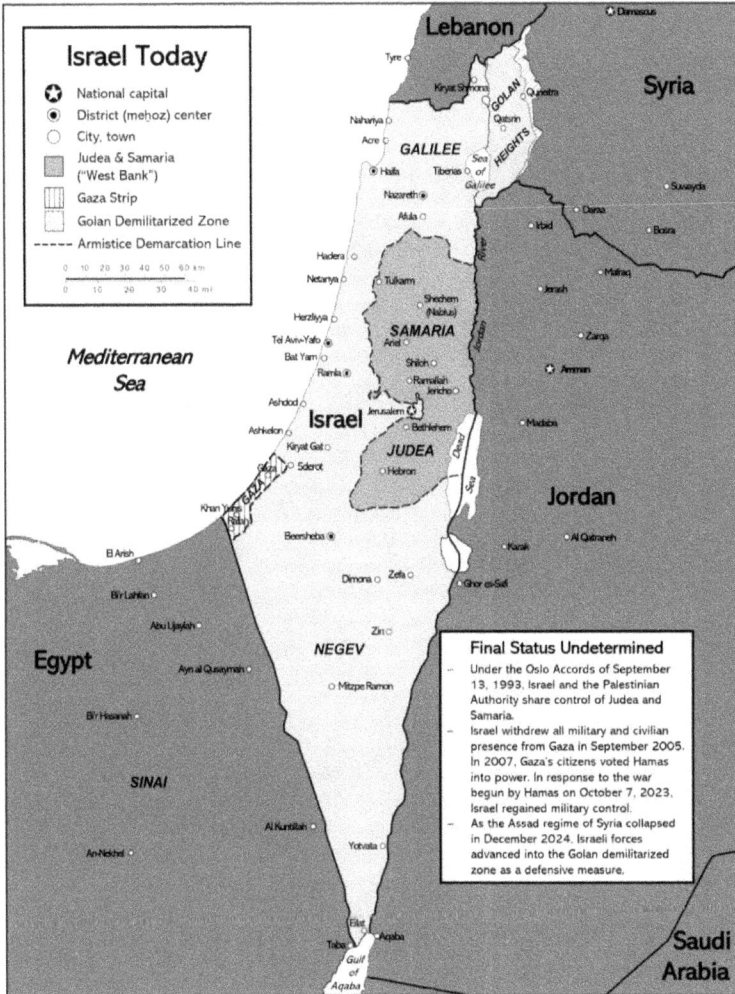

Map 2. Israel Today. (Based on Public Domain map by UN.org, via Wikimedia Commons, https://commons.wikimedia.org/wiki/File:Map_of_Israel,_neighbours_and_occupied_territories.svg.)

INTRODUCTION

WHAT IS ZIONISM AND
WHY DOES IT MATTER?

Why is it controversial to say that the land of Israel belongs to the people of Israel? We can say that Bohemia and Moravia belong to the Czech people, that Tibet belongs to the Tibetan people, and that Mexico belongs to the Mexican people, but for some reason we can't say that Israel belongs to the people of Israel without offending someone.

Maybe it's because Czechs, Tibetans, and Mexicans aren't Jews.

If that is the reason, then we should again ask, why is that? If the Jewish people are the people of Israel, and if the land of Israel has not moved since Bible times, then why can't we say that the Jewish people should live in their ancestral homeland?

That is the basic definition of Zionism.

Those who do not know better might fall for the libelous fantasy that Zionism is somehow a vast Jewish conspiracy that aims to dominate the world. The Anti-Defamation League is one Jewish organization that has been fighting such lies for over a century. According to the ADL, Zionism is simply, "the movement for the self-determination and statehood for the Jewish people in their ancestral homeland, the land of Israel."[1]

The first people who should support the Zionist dream are the Jewish people themselves. They do, in fact. That was the underlying element in a conversation with one of my Jewish Israeli friends about politics in his country. As he explained, except for the Arabs and Marxists

---

1   "Zionism," Anti-Defamation League, September 1, 2016, https://www.adl.org/resources/backgrounder/zionism.

in the Knesset (Israel's parliament), all the other parties and the individual Knesset members are Zionists. That means they share the core value that Israel should continue to exist as the world's only Jewish State and homeland of the Jewish people.[2]

That core value is as true now, at the end of 2024, as it was in 1922, when the League of Nations awarded to Great Britain a Mandate over Palestine to establish a homeland for the Jewish people in such a way that would preserve the civil and religious rights of existing non-Jewish communities living there.[3] That was the intent of the Jewish pioneers who had begun returning to their homeland in the 1880s, when Palestine was still a possession of the Islamic empire of the Ottoman Turks. Their intent was to connect with and expand the Jewish communities that had remained in their homeland from ancient times, not to displace the Arabs and other peoples who had come to live there over the centuries. After 1,900 years of exile, those pioneers were finally able to act on the biblically-inspired dream of the Jewish people to return home to their land, to their holy city of Jerusalem, and to their God who had created them as a nation and given them Eretz Israel (the Land of Israel) as their homeland.

The biblical roots of Zionism should be reason enough for Christians to join with Jews in making the Zionist dream a reality. That was enough for Christian Zionists like Reverend William Hechler, the Anglican clergyman who was instrumental in helping Theodor Herzl, the father of modern Zionism, make connections with the monarchs and power brokers of Europe. Those biblical roots inspired statesmen

---

2   Israeli tour guide Hanoch Young, telephone conversation with Alex David Altman and the author, December 5, 2024.

3   "British Palestine Mandate: Text of the Mandate (July 24, 1922)," Jewish Virtual Library, https://www.jewishvirtuallibrary.org/text-of-the-british-mandate-for-palestine.

like British Prime Ministers David Lloyd George and Winston Churchill, and American Presidents Woodrow Wilson and Harry Truman,
all of whom were instrumental in the rebirth of Israel. The Bible also
inspired ordinary disciples of Jesus like the Ten Boom family of the
Netherlands, who laid down their lives to protect Jews during the Holocaust in their homeland. Their examples further inspired contemporary
Christian Zionists like Dean Bye, who founded Return Ministries to
assist Jews making Aliyah from the former Soviet Union, Tommy Waller,
who founded HaYovel to bring Christian volunteers to Israel to help
Jewish farmers, and Chris Mitchell, who has been reporting news from
Jerusalem for a quarter century as the Middle East Bureau Chief for the
Christian Broadcasting Network (CBN).

These are some of the many Christians who have understood from
their Bibles that the Jewish people and the land of Israel are special to
God, and that the redemption of the whole world is connected to the
return of the Jews to their land. As explained in this volume, what these
Christians have done and are doing in support of Israel and the Jewish
people is linked to the work God has done since antiquity to establish
and preserve his Covenant Nation of Israel as the vehicle of his redemption of all nations.

The biblical foundation of Zionism is the most important reason for
Christians to support Israel, but there are other reasons. The historical
record of the Jewish connection to Eretz Israel is one of those. Another
is the nature of the State of Israel as the only democratic society in the
Middle East. The Jewish State is an expression of the Judeo-Christian
values on which Western Civilization rests, and is a continuation or
resumption of the sovereign exercise of those values on the very land
where they originated. Israel is a source of stability, a champion of
religious freedom, an economic powerhouse, and a voice of tolerance
in a very intolerant neighborhood. These are practical reasons Israel's

neighbors and all nations would find it in their best interests to seek out good relations with Israel, as have the United Arab Emirates and other signatories to the Abraham Accords.

But what does all this have to do with ordinary Christians? Why is it important for a faithful church member in Texas, for example, to care about the Arab-Israeli conflict, and even the existence of Israel as the world's only Jewish state?

Because we are living through the greatest transformation the world has seen since the First World War, a time when God intervened to bring his Jewish children home. How his Christian children respond to that transformation may be the greatest test of our faith since the advent of Christianity.

This transformation first came to my attention in the form of social media images of the largest mass murder of Jews since the Shoa (Holocaust). The world changed on October 7, 2023, when the Islamic Resistance Movement (Hamas) launched its genocidal attacks on Israel. The news impacted me deeply. Years of devotion to cultivating Christian-Jewish relations and Christian support for Israel had made this personal. Because this tragedy had fallen on my friends, it was as if it had fallen on me.

Israelis of all faiths and ethnicities still wrestle with the trauma inflicted on them by the October 7 atrocities and the war those atrocities ignited. I can only imagine how deep that trauma is. It is not only the trauma of a people who have suffered death, destruction, displacement, terror, economic uncertainty, and family separation. It is not only the trauma of a nation grieving over innocent hostages, from babes to elders, held in torturous captivity in Gaza. It is all that and more, because the Jewish people have endured such trauma from generation to generation since they became a people.

I have been to Holocaust sites at Auschwitz, Dachau, Prague, and Cracow, as well as the Holocaust Memorial Museum in Washington, and The World Holocaust Remembrance Center (Yad Vashem) in Jerusalem. I have studied Jewish history from antiquity to the present, and I see how Israel's miraculous rebirth in 1948 literally fulfills Ezekiel's Dry Bones prophecy (Ezekiel 37:1-15). God has done and is doing great things for his Chosen People, but why must those great things come at such great cost?

The images that flooded the world on October 7 brought back memories of what I had seen at those Holocaust sites, and what I had learned about the countless atrocities Jewish people have suffered over the centuries, often at the hands of Christians. Perhaps I was naïve to expect that this new outrage would bring a different response from the Christian world.

The response has been different in the circles I travel. God has been doing something remarkable with Christendom since 1948, and especially since 1967, when Israel regained sovereignty over all Jerusalem and control over the biblical heartland of Judea and Samaria. An eschatological switch flipped with the restoration of the Jewish people to their ancestral homeland. As I have seen with my own eyes, this is prophecy fulfilled, and there is much more fulfillment yet to come.

That, I believe, is why God has visited the Torah Awakening on the church worldwide.[4] Christians have begun to take interest in the Jewish roots of our faith. We are awakening to the realization that Jesus of Nazareth, the one we believe to be the Messiah (Christ) of Israel and the world, was Jewish, that his upbringing was Jewish, and that his

---

4   My friend Rivkah Lambert Adler has documented this global Torah Awakening in her book, *Ten From The Nations: Torah Awakening Among Non-Jews* (Jerusalem, Geula Watch Press, 2022).

worldview and way of thinking was Jewish. The foundation of his world was the Torah—the five books of Moses (Genesis, Exodus, Leviticus, Numbers, Deuteronomy). His teachings were based on the Torah and the rest of the Hebrew Bible (Old Testament), as were the prophecies he and his apostles cited as fulfilled in proof of his messiahship. That is why many Christians now take interest in the Hebrew scriptures and in Jewish biblical understanding so that we may better understand Jesus and follow his example.

This brings us back to the circles in which I travel—circles where Christians actively pray for Israel, cultivate relationships with Jews, study the Bible with Jewish teachers, volunteer to work in Israel, market and buy Israeli-made products, and assist Jewish people in making Aliyah (immigration to Israel). In the prayer meetings and events I regularly attend, Christians exhibit an understanding and appreciation of Shabbat (Sabbath), the Feasts of the Lord such as Passover, Pentecost (Shavuot), and Tabernacles (Sukkot), the Hebrew language, and Jewish commentary on the scriptures. The church where I worship is a Sabbath-keeping Messiaic fellowship. There are many such congregations across the United States and around the world. Most Christians still attend traditional Sunday churches, but there is a growing familiarity with and appreciation of Jewish biblical understanding across the broad spectrum of Christianity.

Such is the impact of the Torah Awakening as I have observed it since 2001. This is a global phenomenon, although it is not a vast popular movement. It seems that a small number of pioneers from both halves of the Covenant Family are marking the path so more can follow in time.

That time may be nearer than we expect. The events of October 7, 2023, may even mark the threshold of that time. Judging from the explosion of antisemitism across the world in the wake of October 7, the loudest voices are those who call for the destruction of the Jewish State and the subjugation of the Jewish people. They do not represent the majority, nor do their shouted slogans invoke true social justice. How can supporters of Arab Palestinian terror and genocide of Jews be connected with any kind of justice? Yet those voices are the loudest. They are accompanied by acts of violence against Jewish people and property, by governmental and private sector censorship of Israel, and by social media and mainstream media promotion of the pro-Hamas, anti-Israel narrative.

Where is the church in all this? Why are Christians silent, for the most part?

Most Christians are indifferent about Israel because they are uninformed. They do not know much about Israel and have had little interaction with Jewish people. Therefore, Israel has little relevance to them. This is the reason for Christian silence and inaction, which has left the field open to those who would have us believe that Zionism is evil, that Jews as Zionists are of the devil, and that the "Zionist entity" (Israel) must be eradicated.

My Jewish friends have noticed this. They understand that most Christians simply do not know what their Bibles say about Israel. If they did, then they would understand that God's Covenant Nation of Israel is central to his plan of redemption for this world. They would also understand that the Jewish people, as the visible remnant of Israel, are heirs to God's promises, and as such are agents of his redemptive plan.

Israel is Zion, and God is a Zionist. More accurately, Zion is a synonym for Jerusalem, the city King David established as the capital of the united Kingdom of Israel, and which God chose as his holy city (2 Samuel 5:7, 1 Kings 8:1, Psalm 132:13-14). By extension, Zion means the whole land of Israel, which God promised to the Patriarch Abraham and his descendants forever (Genesis 12:7, 13:14-15).

WHAT IS ZIONISM AND WHY DOES IT MATTER?

Christian Zionism is based on the fundamental definition of Zionism: the return of the Jewish people to their homeland and the resumption of Jewish sovereignty in the Land of Israel. The Jewish Virtual Library provides an expanded definition:

> The term "Zionism" was coined in 1890 by Nathan Birn-baum. Its general definition means the national movement for the return of the Jewish people to their homeland and the resumption of Jewish sovereignty in the Land of Israel. Since the establishment of the State of Israel in 1948, Zionism has come to include the movement for the development of the State of Israel and the protection of the Jewish nation in Israel through support for the Israel Defense Forces. From inception, Zionism advocated tangible as well as spiritual aims. Jews of all persuasions – left, right, religious and secular – formed the Zionist movement and worked together toward its goals. Disagreements in philosophy led to rifts in the Zionist move-ment over the years, and a number of separate forms emerged. Notably: Political Zionism; Religious Zionism; Socialist Zionism and Territorial Zionism.[5]

By its very nature, Christian Zionism is a religious, or spiritual, movement. Those who embrace it are Christians who believe the prom-ises of God regarding the Jewish people and the nation of Israel.

In recent decades, Christian Zionism has become a sizable move-ment among Evangelical Christians, but it is not a new phenomenon. Christians have extended aid and support to the Jewish people for centu-

---

5   "A Definition of Zionism," Jewish Virtual Library, https://www.jewishvirtuallibrary.org/a-definition-of-zionism.

8   ALBERT JACKSON MCCARN

ries, although often as lone voices crying out against antisemitic policies, decrees, laws, and doctrines of governments and churches. Beginning in the 19th century, however, Christians began to answer the call of God to assist his Chosen People in their return to the Promised Land of Israel.

The common bond linking Christian Zionists across the ages and across continents is the expectation that the God of Israel will keep his promises to restore his people and his Covenant Nation of Israel in the land he gave them. Moreover, Christian Zionists realize that they, along with their Jewish counterparts, are the agents through whom God is bringing his promises to fulfillment.

Consider this book an invitation to you, dear reader. Will you join your Christian Zionist brothers and sisters in making God's redemptive plans for Israel and the nations a reality in our time?

If you have never considered this question, and still wonder how the Jewish people and the nation of Israel matter to Christians, then read on.

CHAPTER 1
BECAUSE OUR MESSIAH IS JEWISH

One quiet afternoon at the Alamo, two of us tour guides had an engaging conversation about religion. My colleague had grown up Catholic, but wasn't particularly observant. However, he recognized something different in my faith walk that made it difficult to place in any denominational category. He knew I had grown up Protestant, but that I worshipped on Saturday instead of Sunday, and had been a member of a Messianic Jewish congregation. I wasn't Jewish, but I wasn't exactly Christian by any definition he understood, and it puzzled him.

I told my friend that our family had come to recognize the Jewishness of Jesus, and that inspired us to live our faith walk as close as we could to his example. While he didn't entirely agree with our choice, my friend did understand and appreciate it. Then he told me an instructive story.

When he was a boy, my colleague said that he and a friend sat together in a tree talking about the important things in the lives of ten-year-old boys. As their conversation drifted into the topic of religion, my friend made the casual observation that Jesus was Jewish. That came as a shock to his friend. He had never heard such a thing, and it made him angry to think that the Jesus he learned about in church could be a Jew. In tears, he ran home and told his mother. She then called my friend's mother and demanded he stop telling lies about Jesus to her son.

All it takes is a little knowledge of the Bible to realize the ethnic and religious identity of Jesus. Apparently, this little boy's mother, and presumably his father, didn't have much knowledge of the Bible, and weren't taught that key point about our Savior in church. It makes me wonder how much, or how little, Christians really know about our Lord.

It's not a surprise that Jews don't know much about Jesus. As one of my Jewish friends says, they believe Christians are all Medieval Catholics. The nuances of Christian denominations and the history of the church mean nothing to the average Jewish person. What they know of Jesus is distilled from their history of persecution by Christians, and through the lens of popular culture in which the birth of Christ takes second place to presents delivered by a jolly fat man in a red suit who drives a sleigh pulled by flying reindeer. To them, Jesus is a foreign god, far removed from the God of Abraham, Isaac, and Jacob.

Those perceptions make the testimony of one Messianic Jewish leader so powerful. As I heard him tell it, he decided one day to read the New Testament. I don't recall what moved him to pick up the Christian scriptures, but I remember his account of what happened when he did. On reading the first verse of Matthew, "The book of the genealogy of Jesus Christ, the son of David, the son of Abraham," he put down the book and exclaimed, "My God! He was Jewish!"

Why is this a surprise? We sing Christmas carols about Jesus being the King of Israel. Those lyrics are taken from Bible passages every Christian hears at Christmas—passages like these:

> Now after Jesus was born in Bethlehem of Judea in the days
> of Herod the king, behold, wise men from the east came to
> Jerusalem, saying, "Where is he who has been born king of
> the Jews? For we saw his star when it rose and have come
> to worship him." When Herod the king heard this, he was
> troubled, and all Jerusalem with him; and assembling all the
> chief priests and scribes of the people, he inquired of them
> where the Christ was to be born. They told him, "In Bethle-
> hem of Judea, for so it is written by the prophet: 'And you, O
> Bethlehem, in the land of Judah, are by no means least among

the rulers of Judah; for from you shall come a ruler who will
shepherd my people Israel.'"
—Matthew 2:1-6 (quoting Micah 5:2)

And when the time came for their purification according
to the Law of Moses, they brought him up to Jerusalem to
present him to the Lord (as it is written in the Law of the
Lord, "Every male who first opens the womb shall be called
holy to the Lord") and to offer a sacrifice according to what
is said in the Law of the Lord, "a pair of turtledoves, or two
young pigeons." Now there was a man in Jerusalem, whose
name was Simeon, and this man was righteous and devout,
waiting for the consolation of Israel, and the Holy Spirit was
upon him. And it had been revealed to him by the Holy Spirit
that he would not see death before he had seen the Lord's
Christ. And he came in the Spirit into the temple, and when
the parents brought in the child Jesus, to do for him according
to the custom of the Law, he took him up in his arms and
blessed God and said, "Lord, now you are letting your servant
depart in peace, according to your word; for my eyes have seen
your salvation that you have prepared in the presence of all
peoples, a light for revelation to the Gentiles, and for glory to
your people Israel."
—Luke 2:22-32

Christians should also be familiar with the Roman governor Pontius
Pilate, who asked Jesus whether he was the King of the Jews. Jesus never
denied the title, although according to John's Gospel he said his Kingdom
was not of this world. Apparently, that was enough for Pilate to decide
what to write on the placard that would hang on the cross with Jesus:

> Pilate also wrote an inscription and put it on the cross. It read, "Jesus of Nazareth, the King of the Jews." Many of the Jews read this inscription, for the place where Jesus was crucified was near the city, and it was written in Aramaic, in Latin, and in Greek. So the chief priests of the Jews said to Pilate, "Do not write, 'The King of the Jews,' but rather, 'This man said, I am King of the Jews.'" Pilate answered, "What I have written I have written."
> —John 19:19-23

This should be enough to establish that the biblical record affirms the Jewish identity of Jesus. Christians and Jews as well should be satisfied that this is also the historical record. The reliability of the New Testament as a historical record is beyond dispute, regardless what one might think of the spiritual content. Jesus' followers certainly believed him to be the Messiah, which means Anointed One, or King of Israel. In his days, Israel consisted of the Jewish people living in Judea, Galilee, and abroad. The non-Jewish tribes of Israel had long been scattered and lost, although hope still remains that the Messiah will regather them and restore them to the nation. The important point in the First Century, and today, is that the Jewish people comprise the remnant of God's Covenant Nation of Israel. Jews and Romans both considered Jesus to be part of that nation and therefore Jewish.

There should not be any question about the identity of our Savior. That's why there is no irony in Jews defending the Jewishness of Jesus even though they do not accept him as Messiah. Jewish defenders of Jesus are doing what Christians should be doing: relying on historical truth to combat the blatant antisemitism of those who claim that Jesus was born in Palestine and therefore was Palestinian rather than Jewish.[1]

A pastor friend of mine had a personal revelation about Jesus' Jewishness when he visited Israel. At the Kotel (Western Wall of the Temple Mount) in Jerusalem, he observed the Orthodox Jewish men at prayer. They spoke Hebrew, and each man wore a *kippah* (yarmulke, or skullcap) or other suitable head covering. Many of them were wrapped in *tefillin* (phylacteries, leather boxes containing parchment inscribed with verses from the Torah, fastened with straps wrapped around the right arm or head). Most of the men also wore their *tallits* (prayer shawls), and most also had their *tzitzit* (tassels) visible at their waists to remind them and others of God and his commandments (Numbers 15:37-41; Deuteronomy 22:12). As my pastor friend soaked in the scene, he realized that Jesus would have looked, sounded, and acted a lot more like those Jewish men than like him.

This revelation has been sweeping through the church for two generations. The revelation of our Messiah's Jewishness is both a cause and an effect of the Torah Awakening—the recognition that the Torah (usually called the Law) and everything else in the Old Testament have application to Christians because we have professed our faith in the Messiah of Israel and the world. In other words, since we have proclaimed allegiance to the King of Israel, we are motivated to learn the ways of his Kingdom, which are written in the Torah. By logical extension, since the Jewish

---

1   "The myth that Jesus was Palestinian, a ploy designed to invite Christians to support Palestinian nationalism, often morphs into deliberate efforts to deny Jews their history, indigeneity, and right to sovereignty in Israel. Ironically, as Jews seek to combat rising antisemitism, now might be a good time to set the record straight on Christianity's most important figure." Jordan Cope, "Jesus was not Palestinian, we need to dispel that myth forever – opinion," *Jerusalem Post*, December 24, 2023, https://www.jpost.com/opinion/article-779313.

people have faithfully kept the Torah as best they can, preserving the language and customs of God's ancient Covenant people, it makes sense to cultivate relationships with them to learn what they know and expand our understanding of God's entire word.

Thanks to the Torah Awakening, Christians are becoming aware of many features of religious expression that, until recently, were considered exclusively Jewish. Those features include the seventh day Sabbath (Shabbat) and the biblical Feasts of the Lord such as Passover, Pentecost (Shavuot), and Tabernacles (Sukkot). Some Christians have begun observing these special times, as well as other practices like making challah (traditional Shabbat bread), abstaining from foods like pork and shellfish that the Torah says are not for human consumption, and wearing *tzitzit*. They are inspired to do so because they seek to follow the example of their Jewish Messiah. Many now study Torah with rabbinic commentaries from Jewish teachers, not in the interest of converting or being converted, but in the interest of deepening their understanding of the scriptures and investigating the common aspects of our faith. Many others have become familiar with and even accepting of Jewish observance, while retaining traditional Christian times of worship and celebration.

The Torah Awakening has, quite naturally, caused some suspicion and even resistance, being viewed by some as a form of cultural appropriation. However, a growing number of observant Jews now recognize that Christians who understand the Jewishness of their Messiah also want to know and honor his Jewish kin. This has opened avenues of cooperation and understanding between the two halves of God's Covenant People not seen since the First Century, if at all. Christians who honor the Jewish identity of Jesus also honor the Jewish people and support the Jewish State of Israel out of love for them.

CHAPTER 2

BECAUSE THE BIBLE SAYS SO

For the first 40 years of my life, the book of Romans only had 13 chapters. Actually, it did have all 16 chapters, but I can't remember paying attention to Romans 9, 10, and 11 until one evening when a Messianic Jewish brother walked me through those chapters. His friendly instruction revolutionized my understanding of Christian-Jewish relations. That change in perspective brought new context to a passage Christians often cite as the reason they, their churches, and their nations should support Israel:

> Now the LORD said to Abram [later named Abraham], "Go from your country and your kindred and your father's house to the land that I will show you. And I will make of you a great nation, and I will bless you and make your name great, so that you will be a blessing. I will bless those who bless you, and him who dishonors you I will curse, and in you all the families of the earth shall be blessed."
> —Genesis 12:1-3

The way I often hear this passage referenced is in connection to how the United States should maintain a supportive policy toward the State of Israel. What American Christians mean is that they want their nation to be blessed because America provides military assistance, economic support, diplomatic top cover, and freedom of action to the Jewish State. When that is not the case, Christians pray for the hearts of their leaders to be turned back to Jerusalem so that they will not be found fighting against God's plans of restoration for Israel and the Jewish people.

These are the kinds of prayers I have heard not only from American Christians, but from Christians of many nations. All of them take seriously this word of God that he chose Abraham and his descendants (meaning Israel) to be his vehicle of redemption for the whole world. As a result, they believe that God's blessings extend not only to Abraham's seed but also to all who help Israel in fulfilling its divine destiny. That means not only standing with Israel, but also standing against those who actively and passively seek Israel's harm.

The application of God's blessing and cursing extends beyond the national level, but let's stay there for a bit. Several American examples come to mind, all of which could be dismissed by those who choose to do so. As with all things related to our Creator, perceiving his hand at work is largely a matter of whether one is disposed to perceive it. Those who expect him to be involved in human affairs are quick to give him praise, regardless of whether the circumstances work out as they desire, simply because of their faith in him and the testimony of his presence in their lives. Those who doubt whether there is a God or question whether he is active in guiding human actions are more likely to look for other causes to explain away the possibility of divine intervention. That's not a modern phenomenon. As Jesus explained, if people aren't willing to accept the witness of scripture, then they won't believe even if someone were to come back from the dead (Luke 16:31).

The first American example occurred in 1948. That tumultuous year witnessed the beginning of the Cold War, with the inception of the Marshall Plan to rebuild America's allies in Europe, the Berlin Blockade by the Soviet Union, and the Berlin Airlift to supply the city and keep it from falling into Soviet hands. In the Middle East, the British Mandate over Palestine ended as promised with the unilateral withdrawal of British forces on May 14, and the immediate declaration of Israel's independence.

This is where God's promise of blessing comes into play: against the counsel of his advisors, President Harry Truman extended American recognition to the new Jewish State. It was a highly controversial decision for the same reasons any such decision about Israel is considered controversial:

- It upsets the status quo.
- It endangers relations with the Arabs and risks them cutting off our supply of oil.
- It might lead to war.
- It will lead to American isolation because the rest of the world opposes favorable action toward Israel.
- It isn't the right time. Wait for a better opportunity when things are stable.
- It's a political risk in an election year.

These are sound reasons based on political, economic, diplomatic, military, intelligence, and security analyses of observable circumstances. That's why world leaders—especially American and British—have come up with the same answers to the Arab-Israeli conflict for over a century. It's also why they have consistently failed to achieve lasting peace in the Middle East.

These were not the only factors Harry Truman had to consider. His Christian faith and knowledge of the Bible made him receptive to the pleas of his Jewish friend, Eddie Jacobson, to do something for the Jewish people as they desperately sought to rise from the calamity of the Holocaust. That's why Truman agreed to meet with Chaim Weizmann, the future first president of Israel. That pivotal meeting persuaded him that recognizing Israel's independence was the right thing to do, regardless of what the experts told him.[1]

It seems that God responded to Truman's blessing of Israel. Six months later, Truman surprised the world by winning the 1948 presidential election, even though he was projected to lose decisively to New York Governor Thomas E. Dewey. Under Truman's leadership for the next four years, the United States rose in power as leader of the Free World against Soviet communism while engaging in significant transformation through the beginning of the Civil Rights Movement. The world might have been very different had Dewey won the presidency, and while Truman's tenure was far from perfect, his decision to bless Israel resulted in reciprocal blessings both to the United States as a whole and to Truman personally.

The opposite happened in 2005, when Israel unilaterally disengaged from Gaza and from several settlements in Samaria.[2] The disengagement was part of a US-led initiative, a "road map to realize the vision of two States, Israel and Palestine, living side by side in peace and security."[3] The "road map to peace" was the latest in a series of "two-state solution" formulas aimed at achieving lasting peace in the Middle East by establishing Jewish and Arab states on the land previously known as Palestine.

---

1   Risto Huvila, "Harry Truman, Bible-believing president, enabled 'Exodus' 75 years ago," *Jerusalem Post*, April 13, 2022, https://www.jpost.com/christianworld/article-704006; Timothy Bella, "Before the U.S. recognized Israel, a president's friend pushed the cause," *Washington Post*, October 17, 2023, https://www.washingtonpost.com/history/2023/10/17/us-israel-biden-truman-history/.

2   Samaria, Judea, and East Jerusalem comprise the biblical heartland of Israel. The world has incorrectly referred to them as the "West Bank" since 1950, when the Kingdom of Jordan unilaterally annexed them.

3   United Nations Security Council, *A Performance-based Road Map to a Permanent Two-State Solution to the Israeli-Palestinian Conflict*, April 30, 2003, https://peacemaker.un.org/en/node/8984.

President George W. Bush presided over the road map initiative as the key component of his Middle East policy. The road map established an ambitious goal of achieving a final agreement in 2005—just over two years after its adoption by the Quartet of the United States, Russia, the European Union, and the United Nations. It did not work out as planned, largely because Prime Minister Ariel Sharon of Israel had his hands full dealing with the Second Intifada. That Arab terrorist uprising resulted from Palestinian Authority (PA) rejection of the peace agreement President Bill Clinton attempted to achieve at Camp David in July 2000. By the time it ended in February 2005, the Intifada claimed the lives of over a thousand Israelis and nearly 3,500 Arabs.[4]

Sharon resisted efforts by the US-led Quartet to undermine Israel's security position in the midst of terrorist violence not only in Judea, Samaria, and Gaza, but also in Jerusalem and the rest of Israel. The Bush Administration was decisively engaged with wars in Afghanistan and Iraq, as well as anti-terrorist operations across the globe. Nevertheless, it still pressured Israel to proceed with disengagement from Gaza and the Samarian settlements by the deadline of August 2005. The last of the 9,000 Israeli citizens were removed from their homes by August 23, and on September 12 the Israel Defense Force completed its withdrawal from Gaza.[5]

---

4   The PA claimed that the Intifada was in response to future Prime Minister Ariel Sharon's ascent of the Temple Mount in Jerusalem on September 29, 2000. However, the uprising had been planned as early as July of that year, when PA leader Yassir Arafat rejected the Israeli offer of land for peace at the Camp David Summit. "The Second Intifada 2000," *Anti-Defamation League*, September 1, 2016, https://www.adl.org/resources/backgrounder/second-intifada-2000.

5   "Israel's Disengagement from Gaza and North Samaria (2005)," *Israel Ministry of Foreign Affairs*, November 14, 2021, https://www.gov.il/en/pages/israel-s-disengagement-from-gaza-and-north-samaria.

At the same time, the US suffered the worst natural disaster on record. Hurricane Katrina crossed the Gulf Coast on August 29 as a Category 4 hurricane, and wrought havoc on Louisiana, Mississippi, and Alabama. The city of New Orleans was inundated with water, forcing the evacuation of hundreds of thousands of residents.

Is there a connection between American pressure on Israel to withdraw from Gaza and northern Samaria, and the cataclysmic impact of Hurricane Katrina? Could it be an example of God cursing those who curse Abraham's seed? It is plausible. Journalist Bill Koenig makes a strong case for this conclusion.[6] He has made a career of documenting parallels between US policy toward Israel and positive or negative impacts on the US as a result. We may debate Koenig's conclusions, but the volume of data he has compiled over the years indicates there is more to US-Israel relations than standard statecraft.

One additional example is enough for now. In January 2021, as President Donald Trump was leaving office, the White House published a lengthy list of his administration's accomplishments.[7] The list included astounding economic growth, historic trade deals, American energy independence, tax credits and other actions in support of American families, security of the southern border, revitalization of the US military, and restoration of US leadership abroad. These accomplishments ensured Trump's popularity among voters, even in the face of tremendous opposition.

Christians and Jews who appreciate Trump's accomplishments are inclined to point toward divine intervention as a factor, particularly

---

6   Bill Koenig, "Hurricane Katrina: Incredible Parallels Between Israel and the U.S. Evacuations," *Koenig World Watch Daily*, https://watch.org/eye-to-eye/hurricane-katrina-incredible-parallels-between-israel-and-us-evacuations-bill-koenig.

7   "Trump Administration Accomplishments," *The White House*, January 2021, https://trumpwhitehouse.archives.gov/trump-administration-accomplishments/.

because of his favorable policy toward Israel. Under his administration, the US:

- Withdrew from the Joint Comprehensive Plan of Action (JCPOA), commonly called the Iran nuclear deal, in May 2018, and later reinstated economic sanctions against Iran.
- Recognized Jerusalem as the capitol of Israel and moved the American Embassy to Jerusalem on May 14, 2018.
- Acknowledged Israel's sovereignty over the Golan Heights in March 2019.
- Declared in November 2019 that Israeli settlements in Judea and Samaria are not inconsistent with international law.
- Brokered the Abraham Accords, establishing peace between Israel and Bahrain and the United Arab Emirates in September 2020. Morocco and Sudan joined the Accords prior to Trump leaving office.

Could it be that Trump's favorable policies toward Israel—especially his acknowledgment of Jerusalem as Israel's capitol—invoked the blessing of God to ensure his many successes at home and abroad? If so, then why was he not returned to office in the election of 2020? Could his administration have done something against Israel that might have invoked a negative response from the Almighty?

Two things come to mind. The first is the Trump Administration's emphasis on a two-state solution. On January 28, 2020, Trump announced the "Deal of the Century." The plan offered the Palestinians an independent state on a truncated portion of Judea and Samaria, which left many Israeli communities isolated as enclaves within Palestinian territory. However, the plan did include a provision for Israel to assert sovereignty over part of Judea and Samaria. US Ambassador to

Israel David Friedman and Secretary of State Mike Pompeo met with President Trump on June 23 to present the case for American support of the sovereignty plan. According to Friedman, Trump initially seemed favorable, but after encountering opposition from world leaders and American politicians, he decided against it.[8]

Friedman relates that the Covid-19 pandemic was one of the many issues weighing on the President's mind at the time. The World Health Organization declared Covid-19 a Public Health Emergency of International Concern on January 30, just two days after Trump's announcement of the Deal of the Century. The Covid pandemic brought a halt to the surging US economy and was arguably the key component to Trump's loss in the 2020 presidential election.

Did God consider Trump's support of a two-state solution and postponement of supporting Israeli sovereignty in Judea and Samaria as a curse on his chosen people and beloved land? If so, could that be the reason Trump experienced unabated—even unprecedented—opposition throughout his presidency and lost the 2020 election even though he remained very popular with American voters? These are questions Christians should prayerfully consider.

Here are a few other questions Christians should consider:

- Is God finished with Israel and the Jewish people? Has the church replaced them in God's esteem and plan of redemption?
- Does God still care about Jerusalem and the land of Israel?
- Does Israel still exist, or are the Jewish people of today simply a different ethnic group masquerading as Israel?

---

8   David Friedman, *One Jewish State: The Last, Best Hope to Resolve the Israeli-Palestinian Conflict* (West Palm Beach, FL: Humanix Books, 2024), 11-13.

- Is the land called Israel today really the land of Israel, or is it the ancestral home of another people called Palestinians?
- What is the proper Christian attitude toward Israel and the Jewish people? What pleases our God in this regard?

This is where we return to that eye-opening conversation with my Messianic Jewish friend about Romans 9, 10, and 11. Until that time, I was favorable toward Israel and the Jewish people, but had no understanding of God's regard for them or how I should relate to them, other than to pray that Jews have their eyes opened to recognize Jesus as their Messiah. That's probably where most Christians are on this topic.

Sadly, antisemitism is a common feature of Christianity. It's been there ever since the Gentile church and the Jewish remnant of Israel went separate ways. Within a century after Jesus ministered in Jerusalem, Judea, and Samaria, the Romans had defeated the Jews in two wars, destroyed the Temple and the city of Jerusalem, slaughtered hundreds of thousands of Jews, and dispersed multitudes more throughout the Empire. Early church fathers considered these developments as proof that God had cursed the Jewish people because they had killed Christ. They reasoned that the Gentile church, having accepted Christ, assumed the former position of the Jewish people and became the "new Israel" or "spiritual Israel." That is the basic tenet of replacement theology, an erroneous construct that has become a central aspect of all forms of Christianity.[9]

---

9   The spread of replacement theology as a core characteristic of Christianity in all its forms, and the resulting negative impact on Christian-Jewish relations, is well documented. See Bob O'Dell and Ray Montgomery, *The LIST: Persecution of Jews By Christians Throughout History* (Jerusalem: Root Source Press, 2019). For a thorough theological explanation of Replacement Theology and its alternatives, see John Parsons, "Israel and the Church – Understanding Some Theological Options," *Hebrew for Christians*, 2005, https://www.

Is that what God intended? Not many Christians thought about that before 1948 when Israel miraculously returned to life as an independent nation. The equally miraculous liberation of Jerusalem, Judea, Samaria, Gaza, the Golan Heights, and the Sinai Peninsula in the 1967 Six-Day War caused many Christians to revisit their received understanding of where the Jewish people stood in God's eyes. They did not have to look far. Jesus himself had something to say about it:

> You worship what you do not know; we worship what we
> know, for salvation is from the Jews.
> —John 4:22

If Jesus, the object of Christian veneration, gave honor to his Jewish brethren as the channel of salvation, then what else is there about the Jews that we might have missed? Paul spells it out in his letter to the Romans:

> Then what advantage has the Jew? Or what is the value of
> circumcision? Much in every way. To begin with, the Jews were
> entrusted with the oracles of God.
> —Romans 3:1-2

> For I could wish that I myself were accursed and cut off from
> Christ for the sake of my brothers, my kinsmen according to
> the flesh. They are Israelites, and to them belong the adoption,
> the glory, the covenants, the giving of the law, the worship,
> and the promises. To them belong the patriarchs, and from
> their race, according to the flesh, is the Christ, who is God

---

hebrew4christians.com/Articles/Israel/israel.html#loaded.

over all, blessed forever. Amen.

—Romans 9:3-5

Paul's essay in Romans 9-11 is all about how the Jewish people are still part of God's plan of redemption and how Gentile Christians should relate to them. He writes about a "partial hardening" or "blindness in part" that has happened to Israel "until the fullness of the Gentiles has come in." That doesn't mean God has tossed the Jewish people out of his Covenant Nation and cursed them forever. Far from it! On the contrary, as Paul reasons, God has established conditions by which foreigners from the nations can be included in the covenant of redemption he made with Abraham and extended to Abraham's children of Israel. That is why Paul exhorts his Roman readers (and us) that they should not be arrogant toward the root of Israel that supports both them and their Jewish brethren (Romans 11:13-18).

Paul's message takes nothing away from the good news that we are all saved by grace through faith in the Messiah. Rather, he speaks to some still-mysterious elements in the work of Messiah. God's covenant with Israel somehow remains intact, and the Jewish people, as the visible remnant of Israel, continue to be part of it. How this is possible despite their not accepting Jesus in the way Christians expect remains a profound mystery. That crucial question is one we shall have to set aside for the moment. For now, we should simply soak in Paul's assertion that "all Israel will be saved" and that "the gifts and the calling of God are irrevocable" (Romans 11:29).

How can Paul be so certain that God still loves the Jewish people? How is it that this message seems to have escaped the church for so many centuries? Maybe the answer is in Bible knowledge—specifically, in what Paul understood, but most Christians throughout history have not. As a highly trained Jewish scholar, Paul understood what God had declared through Moses and the Prophets. That's why he quoted Isaiah 59:20-21 and Jeremiah 31:33-34 as proof texts for his assertion that all Israel will be saved. However, since those texts are part of the Old Testament, Christians are less familiar with them, and less likely to view them with the same regard as New Testament texts.

Is there anything else in the New Testament that testifies to the validity of God's continued calling on Israel and the Jewish people? There is the testimony of our Savior:

> Do not think that I have come to abolish the Law or the
> Prophets; I have not come to abolish them but to fulfill them.
> For truly, I say to you, until heaven and earth pass away, not
> an iota, not a dot, will pass from the Law until all is accom-
> plished.
> —Matthew 5:17-18

The Law and the Prophets is a reference to the Old Testament. Jesus says he did not come to nullify those writings, but to fulfill them.[10] That means they remain in effect as long as heaven and earth exist—which is another Old Testament reference. Moses invoked those same two witnesses when he presented God's Covenant to Israel:

> I call heaven and earth to witness against you today, that I have
> set before you life and death, blessing and curse. Therefore
> choose life, that you and your offspring may live, loving the
> LORD your God, obeying his voice and holding fast to him,
> for he is your life and length of days, that you may dwell in

---

10   For a scholarly treatment of this passage, see David Wilber, *How Jesus Fulfilled the Law: A Pronomian Pocket Guide to Matthew 5:17-20* (Clover, SC: Pronomian Publishing, 2024).

the land that the LORD swore to your fathers, to Abraham, to
Isaac, and to Jacob, to give them."
—Deuteronomy 29:19-20

In that same message, Moses prophesied that God would return
Israel to the Promised Land even after they had rejected him, walked
away from his covenant, and suffered his judgment for their rebellion
(Deuteronomy 30:1-6). That's what we are seeing in our day, as the
Jewish remnant of Israel is back in the land, even in all their secularism
and imperfection.

God is not finished with the Jewish people or the land of Israel.
He still cares what the world thinks about them and does to them. The
Bible is full of God's declarations and promises on that subject.[11] As
Zechariah says, he is jealous for Zion and will again choose Jerusalem
(Zechariah 1:17). That makes God the ultimate Zionist. If God is a
Zionist, shouldn't we also be Zionists?

---

11 See, for example, Leviticus 26:44-45, Isaiah 54:4-8, Jeremiah 23:5-8, Jeremiah 32:36-41,
    Ezekiel 39:25-29, and Zechariah 8:1-8.

CHAPTER 3

BECAUSE GOD PROMISED THE LAND TO ISRAEL

Jesus' parting words before his ascension have inspired his followers for two millennia:

> But you will receive power when the Holy Spirit has come upon you, and you will be my witnesses in Jerusalem and in all Judea and Samaria, and to the end of the earth.
>
> —Acts 1:8

Christians of all streams, including Messianic believers, regard this verse as a job description made possible by the gift of the Holy Spirit. That's the emphasis I usually hear in teachings from this text. Some messages cover the geographic aspect, demonstrating how the expansion of the Early Church was exactly as Jesus directed: from Jerusalem to Judea, then to Samaria, and then to the ends of the earth.

That is historical truth and one of many examples of the Bible's reliability. The places mentioned in the Bible are real, and the events recorded in it really happened (see Map 3, Palestine in the Time of Jesus). That's the consistent position Christians have held, citing historical truths as evidence of the Bible's inspiration by God and its continued relevance. However, Christian faith in the Bible as the inspired word of God would be much more effective if it were accompanied by an understanding of geography. It seems that few people know what those ancient biblical places are called today and where to find them on a map.

Map 3. Palestine in the Time of Jesus. (Charles Foster Kent, Palestine in the time of Jesus, 4 B.C. - 30 A.D.: including the period of Herod, 40 - 4 B.C. [S.l.: s.n, 1912] Map. https://www.loc.gov/item/2009579463/.)

That explains an awkward moment at church when I asked a friend whether the Jewish people should be allowed to live in the West Bank. I was surprised when my friend responded, "I don't have enough information to answer that question."

That's not what I expected from an accomplished Bible teacher and a person who genuinely loves Jesus. I appreciate my friend's honesty, but the answer is alarming. It means this mature Christian doesn't know that the modern invented name "West Bank" refers to Jerusalem, Judea, and Samaria—the very places where Jesus told his followers they would be his witnesses.

Jesus mentioned those places because they are the heartland of God's Covenant Nation of Israel. In his day, as in ours, the Jewish people were the visible remnant of that nation. Much of the world's Jewish population lived in Jerusalem, Israel's eternal capital city, and in Judea. In fact, they are called *Jews* because they come from *Judea*, the land of the Jews. Few, if any, Jews lived in Samaria in Jesus' day, although, like Judea, Samaria has been part of Israel since ancient times. In the first century, Samaria was home to descendants of Israel's conquered and scattered Northern Kingdom who had remained in the land and mixed with other peoples. They are still there to this day, living in a community built around their temple on Mount Gerizim overlooking Shechem (Nablus), where Jesus met the Samaritan woman at the well (John 4).

Jesus and the apostles traveled and ministered throughout Judea and Samaria, both to Jews and non-Jews. It is sacred land to Christians, but it was sacred to Jews long before Jesus was born in Bethlehem of Judea. Many events recorded in the Bible took place in Judea and Samaria, including the stories of the patriarchs Abraham, Isaac, and Jacob; the prophets Elijah, Isaiah, and Jeremiah; and the kings David, Solomon, and Hezekiah. That is why Jerusalem, Judea, and Samaria are the Biblical heartland and the core of the land God gave as an inheritance to Israel.

So how did the Biblical heartland become known as the West Bank? That happened in 1950 when the Kingdom of Jordan annexed the region after Israel's war of independence. That region was to have been part of an Arab state according to the United Nations plan of partition for Palestine in 1947 (see Map 4, Israel's Borders, 1949-1967)."[1] However, the Arabs rejected that plan, as they have rejected every offer of a Palestinian Arab state ever since. The Jewish people of Palestine accepted the plan and, in May 1948, declared independence in the land allocated for a Jewish state. The Arabs then went to war, with the backing of Egypt, Jordan, Syria, Lebanon, Iraq, Saudi Arabia, and Yemen, intending to drive the Jews out and occupy all the land. Even the intervention of sizable forces from the Arab nations could not bring victory, however, and Israel's independence was established.

The war's end left the Jordanian military in control of East Jerusalem, Judea, and Samaria. Rather than create an independent Arab Palestine, the Arabs living there opted to become part of Jordan. In April 1950, the Jordanian Parliament adopted a resolution for, "the complete unity between the East and West Banks of the Jordan and for their union in one state, which is the Hashemite Kingdom of Jordan..." That is how Judea and Samaria became the West Bank. The world continues to use this name even though Israel liberated Jerusalem and gained control of Judea and Samaria in the 1967 Six-Day War, and Jordan relinquished all claims to the land in 1988 (see Map 5, Israel After the Six-Day War, June 5-10, 1967).[2]

---

1   A point that too often escapes notice is that Jews and Arabs living under the British Mandatory Government in Palestine were both called Palestinians. It was only after Israel's independence in 1948 that Jewish Palestinians began to be called Israelis, and the term Palestinian began to be applied solely to Arabs living in the former Mandatory territory.

2   United Nations Committee on the Exercise of the Inalienable Rights of the Palestinian

It should be evident how this name change plays into the political issue of who has title to Judea and Samaria. By calling those regions something other than the historical and biblical names, opponents of the Jewish State of Israel and of Jewish presence in their ancient homeland can build a case that Jews are occupiers of Arab land. Sadly, the people who should be most supportive of the Jewish inheritance of Israel's Biblical heartland are unaware of this issue and, in their ignorance, play right into the hands of Israel's enemies.[3]

The Arabs are not the first to change the name of the Biblical heartland. The Romans did it in the year 135, after the Bar Kokhba Revolt, the last Jewish uprising against Rome. In retaliation, Emperor Hadrian renamed Judea "Syria Palaestina," which became the familiar term "Palestine." That name referred to the ancient Philistines, who no longer existed as a people.[4] From that time until 1948, Palestine became synonymous with the Holy Land of Israel.

There is nothing new about the efforts of Israel's enemies to oppose Jewish presence in and ownership of the land of Israel. Not long after God promised to make Abraham a nation, he and his nephew, Lot, had to separate because their herdsmen were at odds about access to the land

People, *The Legal Status of The West Bank and Gaza*, January 1, 1982, https://www.un.org/unispal/document/auto-insert-203742/; "Disengagement from the West Bank," The Hashemite Kingdom of Jordan, http://www.kinghussein.gov.jo/his_periods9.html.

3   This is why a concerted effort is needed to educate both Christians and Jews about the truth of Judea and Samaria. For that reason, the National Religious Broadcasters (NRB), along with the Israel Allies Foundation, Israel 365, and The Israel Guys published the Biblical Heartland Resolution on February 22, 2024, pledging to drop the name West Bank and use the true names of Judea and Samaria. Maayan Jaffe-Hoffman, "Christian media adopt biblical Judea and Samaria over West Bank." *The Jerusalem Post*, February 22, 2024, https://www.jpost.com/christianworld/article-788363.

4   Douglas J. Feith, "The Forgotten History of the Term 'Palestine,'" *Mosaic Magazine*, December 21, 2021, https://www.hudson.org/node/44363.

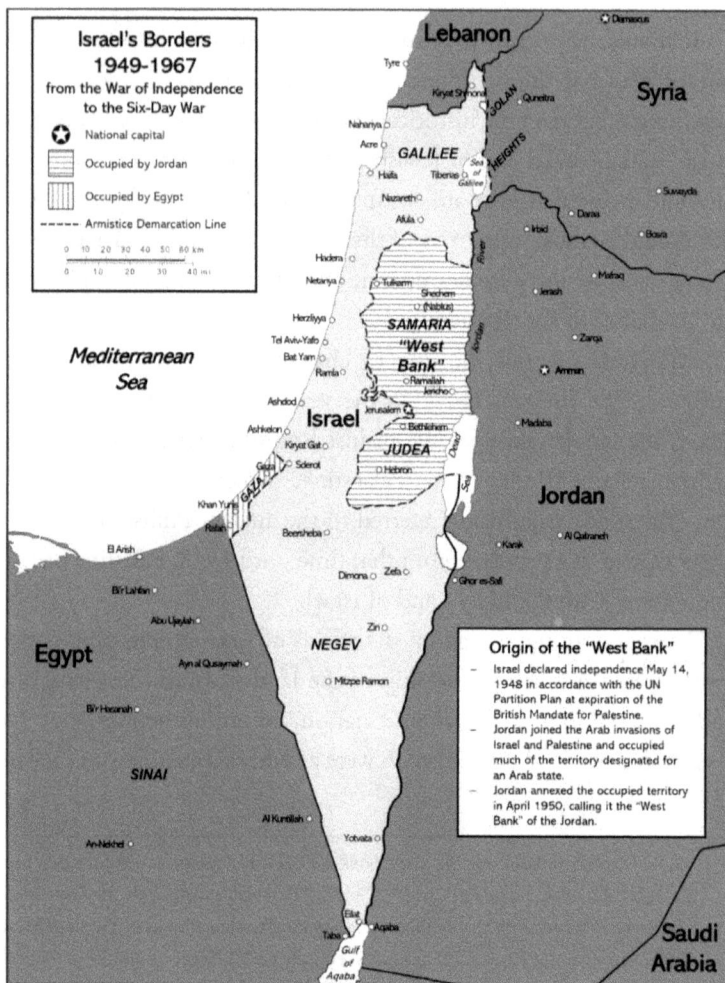

**Israel's Borders
1949-1967**

from the War of Independence
to the Six-Day War

⭐ National capital

▦ Occupied by Jordan

▥ Occupied by Egypt

- - - - Armistice Demarcation Line

0 10 20 30 40 50 80 km

0   10   20   30   40 mi

Lebanon

Damascus

Tyre

Kiryat Shmona

Quneitra

GOLAN HEIGHTS

Syria

Nahariya

Acre

GALILEE

Haifa

Tiberias

Sea of Galilee

Suwayda

Nazareth

Afula

Irbid

Dara

Bosra

Hadera

Netanya

Tulkarm

Shechem (Nablus)

Jenin

Mafraq

Herzliyya

SAMARIA

Tel Aviv-Yafo

Bat Yam

"West Bank"

Zarqa

Ramla

Ramallah

Amman

Jericho

Mediterranean
Sea

Ashdod

Ashkelon

Israel

Jerusalem

Bethlehem

Madaba

Kiryat Gat

JUDEA

Sderot

Hebron

Gaza

GAZA

Khan Yunis

Rafah

Beersheba

Karak

Al Qatraneh

Jordan

El Arish

Dimona

Zefa

Ghor es-Safi

Bir Lahfan

Abu Ujaylah

Zin

NEGEV

Egypt

Ayn al Qusaymah

Mitzpe Ramon

Origin of the "West Bank"

- Israel declared independence May 14, 1948 in accordance with the UN Partition Plan at expiration of the British Mandate for Palestine.
- Jordan joined the Arab invasions of Israel and Palestine and occupied much of the territory designated for an Arab state.
- Jordan annexed the occupied territory in April 1950, calling it the "West Bank" of the Jordan.

Bir Hasanah

SINAI

Al Kuntilah

Yotvata

An-Nakhel

Eilat

Aqaba

Taba

Gulf
of
Aqaba

Saudi
Arabia

Map 4. Israel's Borders, 1949-1967. (Based on Public Domain map by UN.org, via Wikimedia Commons, https://commons.wikimedia.org/wiki/File:Map_of_Israel,_neighbours_and_occupied_territories.svg; Public Domain Map by Honza Havlíček, derived from 1967_Six_Day_War_-_Battle_of_Golan_Heights.jpg: Mr. Edward J. Krasnoborski and Mr. Frank Martini, Department of History, U.S. Military Academy, via Wikimedia Commons, https://commons.wikimedia.org/wiki/File:Israel_1949-1967.svg.)

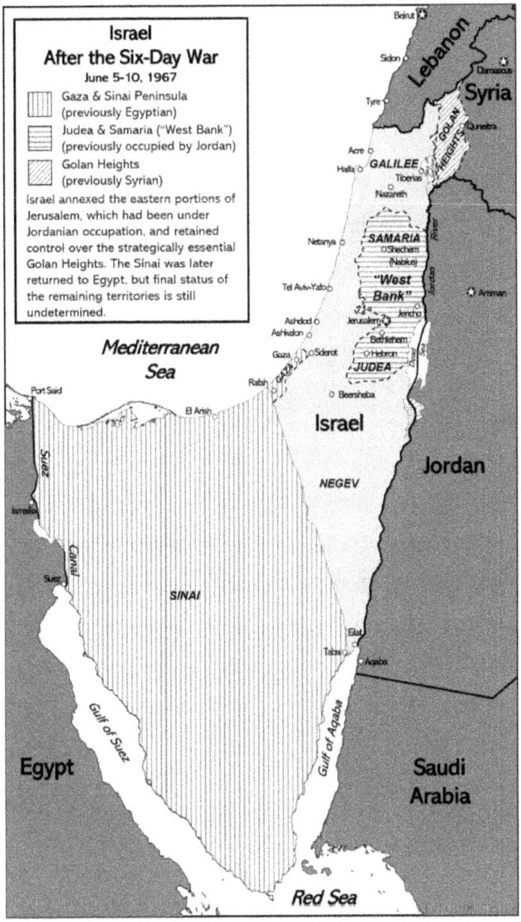

Map 5. Israel After the Six-Day War, June 5-10, 1967. (Based Public Domain Map by Honza Havlíček, derived from 1967_Six_Day_War_-_Battle_of_Golan_Heights.jpg: Mr. Edward J. Krasnoborski and Mr. Frank Martini, Department of History, U.S. Military Academy, via Wikimedia Commons, https://commons.wikimedia.org/wiki/File:Israel_1949-1967.svg: Israel_and_surroundings_location_map.svg: NordNordWestEgypt_location_map.svg: NordNordWestLebanon_location_map.svg: NordNordWest derivative work: Mapeh, CC BY-SA 3.0 https://creativecommons.org/licenses/by-sa/3.0, via Wikimedia Commons, https://upload.wikimedia.org/wikipedia/commons/6/65/Israel_and_surroundings_location_map.svg.)

(Genesis 13). Years later, Sarah, Abraham's wife, demanded he send away his concubine Hagar and her son Ishmael to ensure there would be no rival to her son Isaac (Genesis 21:8-21). In the next generation, Abraham's grandsons, Jacob and Esau, became rivals over the inheritance (Genesis 25:29-34, 27:1-46, 32:1-21, 33:1-20). That rivalry continues to this day, according to Jewish understanding. It's a rivalry that God promises to settle in time when he brings judgment on Esau's descendants, known as Edom.[5]

The dispute between Jacob and Esau, or Israel and Edom, is only one of the sibling rivalries God promises to resolve. Jacob's twelve sons also had trouble getting along, and so did the tribes they fathered. In time, the nation split into two kingdoms because the two leading tribes, Judah and Ephraim, could not resolve their differences. That was the origin of the Jewish kingdom of Judah in the south and the kingdom of Israel centered in Samaria. They fought each other even as the Assyrian Empire encroached on both and finally conquered the northern kingdom.

The bitter irony is that sibling rivalry persisted even in the face of threats by outside enemies to obliterate Abraham's family by assimilating them, conquering them, or driving them off the land. That is the story

---

5   Edom, as well as Moab and Ammon (nations descended from Lot's daughters), existed within the territory of what is now the Kingdom of Jordan. Jewish tradition connects Edom with Rome – both the Roman Empire and Roman Christianity. For a concise rabbinic explanation of that tradition, see Rabbi Elie Mischel, "How Bible Prophecy in Obadiah is Being Fulfilled in Israel Right Now!," Israel Connect, January 7, 2025, educational video, 39:47, https://youtu.be/avgGRY0EbQQ?si=RxLMWlMJOoU6pkKh. See also Yehuda Altein, "14 Facts About Esau Everyone Should Know," Chabad.org, https://www.chabad.org/library/article_cdo/aid/4937157/jewish/14-Facts-About-Esau-Everyone-Should-Know.htm; Richard Gottheil and M. Seligsohn, "Edox, Idumean," The Jewish Encyclopedia, 1906, https://www.jewishencyclopedia.com/articles/5434-edox-idumea; Dr. Malka Z. Simkovich, "Esau the Ancestor of Rome," TheTorah.com, 2018, https://www.thetorah.com/article/esau-the-ancestor-of-rome.

of the entire Bible, including the New Testament. Opposition to Jesus and his followers was but one of many fractures in Jewish society as the nation struggled with the best way to remain true to God's calling while enduring Roman oppression. That was the focus of the debate about Jesus:

> So the chief priests and the Pharisees gathered the council and said, "What are we to do? For this man performs many signs. If we let him go on like this, everyone will believe in him, and the Romans will come and take away both our place and our nation.
> —John 11:48

The Romans eventually did take away the Jews' place and nation, but they could never obliterate the ancient Jewish title to the land. The Bible records four significant real estate transactions of Abraham and his descendants buying the land:

- Abraham's purchase of the Cave of Machpelah as a burial place for Sarah (Genesis 23:1-20). That plot of land is still revered as the Tomb of the Patriarchs in the city of Hebron.
- Jacob's purchase of land near the city of Shechem (Genesis 33:18-20). Jacob gave that land to his son Joseph, and there Joseph's bones were laid to rest (John 4:5-12; Joshua 24:32). Joseph's tomb remains to this day in the city of Nablus, the name of the Arab city on the site of ancient Shechem.
- David's purchase of the threshing floor of Araunah (Ornan) the Jebusite (2 Samuel 24:18-25; 1 Chronicles 21:18-30). That site atop Mount Moriah in Jerusalem is now known as the Temple Mount.

- The prophet Jeremiah's purchase of his cousin's field in their ancestral town of Anathoth (Jeremiah 32:1-15). That purchase was a prophetic act by which God promised to return the exiles of Israel to their homeland. Today, Anathoth is the Arab town of Anat, a suburb of Jerusalem.

No matter how loudly Israel's enemies protest that the Jews have no place in the Promised Land, they cannot erase the fact that their title extends back to the time of Abraham the Hebrew. But why that particular land? What is so special about Israel, and why is it still important that the Jewish people live there? We can start with God's own testimony that the land is special to him:

> But the land that you are going over to possess is a land of
> hills and valleys, which drinks water by the rain from heaven,
> **a land that the LORD your God cares for.** The eyes of the
> LORD your God are always upon it, from the beginning of
> the year to the end of the year.
> —Deuteronomy 11:11-12 (emphasis added)

Israel is God's special land because, according to Jewish tradition, he began forming the earth there. The foundation stone of the world is said to be located on the Temple Mount in Jerusalem, presently under the Muslim shrine, the Dome of the Rock. It was on that site that Abraham bound Isaac and prepared to offer him as a sacrifice according to God's command (Genesis 22). The Holy of Holies of the two Temples were constructed over that stone, and to this day Jews pray toward it in acknowledgment of its sanctity.[6]

---

6   "The Foundation Stone: The Center of Creation," *Jewish Heritage Online Magazine,*

Christians and Jews share the belief that the God of Abraham, Isaac, and Jacob created the world. He must have started somewhere, so why not Jerusalem, the city where he placed his name (1 Kings 9:1-3; Psalm 48:1-2; Zechariah 8:1-3; Matthew 5:35)? Of course, there was no city there at the beginning of the world, but given the history of Jerusalem as a holy city since the days of Abraham (Genesis 14), it is no great leap of faith for those who believe in the biblical account of creation to accept that it all started there.

Even if the Jewish tradition is incorrect, the fact remains that Jerusalem is God's Holy City, and the territory around it is his Holy Land. When he began to redeem this planet, he started right there. Then he chose Abraham to take possession of the Holy Land and build a family and nation to be the instruments of redemption for the whole earth. That's the reason the land and people of Israel have always been special. As Paul writes, "as regards election, they [the Jewish people of Israel] are beloved for the sake of their forefathers" (Romans 11:28).

God's plan of redemption requires his people to be back in his land, with the support of people from all nations. That's why the only time in scripture that God promises to do something with all his heart and soul is in connection to restoring the Jewish people to their ancestral homeland:

https://www.jhom.com/topics/stones/foundation.html#1, accessed August 27, 2024; "The Holy of Holies," *The Temple Institute*, https://templeinstitute.org/illustrated-tour-the-holy-of-holies/, accessed August 27, 2024; Lambert Dolphin, "Early History of the Temple Mount," *The Temple Mount in Jerusalem*, April 9, 1996, https://www.templemount.org/earlytm.html; Joshua Hammer, "What Is Beneath the Temple Mount?" Smithsonian Magazine, April 2011, https://www.smithsonianmag.com/history/what-is-beneath-the-temple-mount-920764/.

> Now therefore thus says the LORD, the God of Israel,
> concerning this city of which you say, 'It is given into the
> hand of the king of Babylon by sword, by famine, and by
> pestilence': Behold, I will gather them from all the countries
> to which I drove them in my anger and my wrath and in great
> indignation. I will bring them back to this place, and I will
> make them dwell in safety. And they shall be my people, and I
> will be their God. I will give them one heart and one way, that
> they may fear me forever, for their own good and the good of
> their children after them. I will make with them an everlasting
> covenant, that I will not turn away from doing good to them.
> And I will put the fear of me in their hearts, that they may not
> turn from me. **I will rejoice in doing them good, and I will
> plant them in this land in faithfulness, with all my heart
> and all my soul.**
> —Jeremiah 32:36-41 (emphasis added)

This is a priority for our Redeemer. A kingdom requires a land, a people, and a king. God is the king, and Messiah Son of David will rule in his name. He will govern his people Israel and all nations from Jerusalem. That's the promise we read in Isaiah:

> It shall come to pass in the latter days That the mountain of
> the house of the LORD shall be established as the highest of
> the mountains, and shall be lifted up above the hills; and all
> the nations shall flow to it, and many peoples shall come, and
> say: "Come, let us go up to the mountain of the LORD, to the
> house of the God of Jacob, that he may teach us his ways and
> that we may walk in his paths." For out of Zion shall go forth
> the law, and the word of the LORD from Jerusalem. He shall

judge between the nations, and shall decide disputes for many peoples; and they shall beat their swords into plowshares, and their spears into pruning hooks; nation shall not lift up sword against nation, neither shall they learn war anymore.

—Isaiah 2:24

This is why the land of Israel is important to Christians. It is not only the historical homeland of the Jewish people, promised to them by God himself, but also it is the land God chose as the place where his restorative justice and government of all the earth originate. This is what Christians uphold when they support the right of the Jewish people to live in their homeland, within the borders God promised to Abraham, Isaac, and Jacob.

CHAPTER 4

BECAUSE GOD'S PROMISES TO ISRAEL ARE ETERNAL

The views from the heights of Elon More are stunning. To the north and east is the Tirzah Valley, connecting the Jordan Valley with Megiddo and the Jezreel Valley. To the west and south are the Mount of Blessing (Mount Gerizim) and Mount of Cursing (Mount Ebal). Israel's twelve tribes stood at those mountains when they had conquered Canaan and pronounced the blessings and curses of God, just as Moses had commanded them (Deuteronomy 27:9-26; Joshua 8:30-35). Nestled between these mountains lies the city of Shechem, whose name means "shoulder." From Elon Moreh, the reason for this name becomes clear: Mount Gerizim and Mount Ebal appear as the shoulders of the ancient city. It's a far more appropriate name than Nablus, which is what the Arabs call it. They took the name from Flavia Neapolis, the name the Roman Emperor Vespasian gave to Shechem in the year 72 after his armies captured the city during the Great Jewish War.

Those are some of the highlights of the views from Elon More, but there is far greater significance to the mountain than panoramic views. On that mountain, 4,000 years ago, God first explained to Abraham why he had called him out of his native land:

> Abram passed through the land to the place at Shechem, to the
> oak of Moreh [Elon More]. At that time the Canaanites were
> in the land. Then the LORD appeared to Abram and said, "To
> your offspring I will give this land." So he built there an altar
> to the LORD, who had appeared to him.
> —Genesis 12:6-7

This promise, given shortly after God's pledge to make Abraham a great nation and to bless all nations through him, highlights the territorial aspect of God's redemptive plan for the world. God reiterated that point not long afterward:

> The LORD said to Abram, after Lot had separated from him,
> "Lift up your eyes and look from the place where you are,
> northward and southward and eastward and westward, for **all
> the land that you see I will give to you and to your offspring
> forever.** I will make your offspring as the dust of the earth,
> so that if one can count the dust of the earth, your offspring
> also can be counted. Arise, walk through the length and the
> breadth of the land, for I will give it to you." So Abram moved
> his tent and came and settled by the oaks of Mamre, which are
> at Hebron, and there he built an altar to the LORD.
> —Genesis 13:14-18 (emphasis added)

When God says "forever," does he really mean for all time, without end? We certainly hope so. If God's "forever" means anything less than forever, then his reliability as Sovereign of the universe is questionable. By extension, that means our eternal destiny is in question.

For Christians, this foundational aspect of our faith begins with the question of whether Jesus Christ is who the scriptures say he is. Our fundamental belief is that he is the Son of God, eternal and equal to the Father. Therefore, just as our Heavenly Father has no beginning and no end, so does the Son. We understand that from scriptures like these:

> Who has performed and done this, calling the generations
> from the beginning? I, the LORD, the first, and with the last;

I am he.
—Isaiah 41:4

Thus says the LORD, the King of Israel And his Redeemer, the LORD of hosts: "I am the first and I am the last; besides me there is no god.
—Isaiah 44:6

I [Jesus] and the Father are one.
—John 10:30

Jesus Christ is the same yesterday and today and forever.
—Hebrews 13:8

"I am the Alpha and the Omega," says the Lord God, "who is and who was and who is to come, the Almighty."
—Revelation 1:8

The key issue is whether we worship an eternal, unchanging Creator, or not. Observant Jews and faithful Christians unanimously answer, "Yes! We serve the God of Abraham, Isaac, and Jacob, who was and is and is to come!"

The next question is whether Jesus Christ is the ultimate expression of the Father in human flesh as the Messiah of Israel and the world. This is where Christians and Jews have our greatest disagreement. Christians have a testimony of the one we call Messiah because it is through him that we have a relationship with God, our Heavenly Father. Jews do not share that testimony, but they do share with Christians the hope of Messiah's coming to rule and reign from Jerusalem and set the nations in order.

For nearly twenty centuries, Christians and Jews have emphasized our disagreement on the identity of the Messiah. That disagreement will be resolved in due time when Messiah is revealed in his fullness and clarifies everyone's understanding. Until then, our course of wisdom is to begin emphasizing the hope we share in what Messiah will do.

This brings us back to the key point that the Messiah adored by Christians is Jewish. That means he is the way by which we from the nations who are not native-born Israelites can enter into that eternal, "forever" covenant that God made with Abraham and his descendants. Abraham was a shepherd, and so was his descendant David. It makes sense, therefore, that David's descendant, Jesus of Nazareth, spoke of himself as the Good Shepherd who would gather the scattered sheep of Israel and bring them all into one sheepfold as one flock (Matthew 10:5-6, 15:24; John 10:14-18).

Jesus made it a point to draw his teachings directly from Moses and the Prophets (the Old Testament). That in itself is reason enough for Christians to study the whole Bible so that we have a better understanding of our Savior's teachings in context. Regarding the Good Shepherd terminology, Jesus drew directly from God's rebuke to the shepherds of Israel in Ezekiel 34. Since those shepherds (Israel's priests, Levites, and kings) had abused the flock and led them astray, God himself promised to shepherd his people. Ezekiel's prophecy concludes with these promises:

> **And I will set up over them one shepherd, my servant David**, and he shall feed them: he shall feed them and be their shepherd. And I, the LORD, will be their God, and my servant David shall be prince among them. I am the LORD; I have spoken. **I will make with them a covenant of peace and banish wild beasts from the land, so that they may dwell**

securely in the wilderness and sleep in the woods. And **I will make them and the places all around my hill a blessing,** and I will send down the showers in their season; they shall be showers of blessing. And the trees of the field shall yield their fruit, and the earth shall yield its increase, and **they shall be secure in their land. And they shall know that I am the LORD, when I break the bars of their yoke, and deliver them from the hand of those who enslaved them.** They shall no more be a prey to the nations, nor shall the beasts of the land devour them. **They shall dwell securely, and none shall make them afraid.** And I will provide for them renowned plantations so that they shall no more be consumed with hunger in the land, and no longer suffer the reproach of the nations. **And they shall know that I am the LORD their God with them, and that they, the house of Israel, are my people, declares the LORD God.** And you are my sheep, human sheep of my pasture, and I am your God, declares the LORD God.

—Ezekiel 34:23-31 (emphasis added)

Notice that God's promise to shepherd Israel is intimately connected to the land of Israel. When God says, "my hill," he is referring to Zion, or Mount Moriah, the site of the Holy Temple in Jerusalem. In this context, God, as Israel's shepherd, intends to make not only his people, but also his land a blessing. This connects the Good Shepherd to God's promise that the land would belong to Abraham and his offspring forever. With this context in mind, look again at the statement Jesus made about his status as shepherd of his people and as coequal with the Father:

> My sheep hear my voice, and I know them, and they follow
> me. I give them eternal life, and they will never perish, and
> no one will snatch them out of my hand. My Father, who has
> given them to me, is greater than all, and no one is able to
> snatch them out of the Father's hand. **I and the Father are
> one.**
> —John 10:27-30 (emphasis added)

The intent here is to demonstrate that God's eternal promises to Abraham apply not only to his physical descendants, the Jewish people of Israel, but also to the spiritual descendants who are adopted into Abraham's family by grace through faith in Israel's Messiah (Ephesians 2:8-13, Galatians 3:29).

Another disconnect between Jews and Christians is the Jewish propensity to emphasize the physical aspects of God's promises, while Christians emphasize the spiritual aspects. Jewish people know that they are the physical descendants of Abraham and heirs to everything God promised, including the land of Israel. Observant Jews understand the direct connection God has with the land and people of Israel.

Christians, on the other hand, have no ancient connection to the land of Israel and have had very little connection to the Jewish people of Israel. Christianity has appropriated the promises God made to Israel, but because there is no connection to the land and people, the church has emphasized the spiritual aspects of those promises and largely ignored the physical aspects.

One example is the popular application of this comforting promise:

> For I know the plans I have for you, declares the LORD, plans
> for welfare and not for evil, to give you a future and a hope.
> Then you will call upon me and come and pray to me, and I

will hear you.

—Jeremiah 29:11

We are quick to turn to this promise as a word of hope in difficult times, claiming it in the expectation that our God will bring good results out of the trials we face. That is a valid interpretation, but Christians who cling to this verse may be surprised to know that it is part of a letter Jeremiah wrote to the Jewish exiles in Babylon. Here it is in context:

> For thus says the LORD: When seventy years are completed for Babylon, I will visit you, and I will fulfill to you my promise and bring you back to this place. For I know the plans I have for you, declares the LORD, plans for welfare and not for evil, to give you a future and a hope. Then you will call upon me and come and pray to me, and I will hear you. **You will seek me and find me, when you seek me with all your heart**. I will be found by you, declares the LORD, and **I will restore your fortunes and gather you from all the nations and all the places where I have driven you**, declares the LORD, and **I will bring you back to the place from which I sent you into exile**.
> —Jeremiah 29:10-14 (emphasis added)

This is a specific promise to the Jewish people of Israel that God will restore them to their land after their time of exile is over. It has application beyond that specific point in history when the Babylonian exile ended because only a fraction of the Jewish exiles returned at that time, and there was yet another and greater exile to happen under the Romans. Christians are not wrong in claiming this promise as part of God's gracious compassion on all his people, but we miss the fullness of the promise if we see it as applying only to individuals and not to the Covenant Nation through which God is bringing redemption to all nations.

Another example comes from Isaiah:

> [N]o weapon that is fashioned against you shall succeed, and you shall refute every tongue that rises against you in judgment. This is the heritage of the servants of the LORD and their vindication from me, declares the LORD.
> —Isaiah 54:17

This word of comfort is another promise made specifically to Israel in the context of God restoring his people in the latter days. God addresses both the land and people of Israel and the city of Jerusalem as a barren widow who shall be restored. They are outcasts because of their rebellion, but he promises to make that right, saying:

> "Fear not, for you will not be ashamed; be not confounded, for you will not be disgraced; for you will forget the shame of your youth, and the reproach of your widowhood you will remember no more. For your Maker is your husband, The LORD of hosts is his name; and the Holy One of Israel is your Redeemer, the God of the whole earth he is called. For the LORD has called you like a wife deserted and grieved in spirit, like a wife of youth when she is cast off, says your God. For a brief moment I deserted you, but with great compassion I will gather you. In overflowing anger for a moment I hid my face from you, but with everlasting love I will have compassion on you," says the LORD, your Redeemer. "This is like the days of Noah to me: as I swore that the waters of Noah should

no more go over the earth, so I have sworn that I will not be angry with you, and will not rebuke you."

—Isaiah 54:4-9

The Lord goes on to say that he will deal with those who continue to condemn his people, and in that context, no weapon formed against them can prosper. Again, the Christian appropriation of this promise is valid, but the promise means more than we have thought. God must be found faithful to his word, and that starts with his word to Abraham. Israel is the national heir to the covenantal promises God made to Abraham, and Israel's people—the native-born and the adopted foreigners—are the individuals entitled to receive those promises.

The argument has been made that God's promises no longer apply to the Jewish people because they, as the native-born Israelites, rebelled against God and were cast out of his covenant. That argument does not stand up against the many scriptures which testify that Israel will rebel and go into exile, but will be restored, and in that restoration, return to God (Deuteronomy 30:1-10, Ezekiel 20:18-38, 37:1-14). All the suffering the Jewish people have endured in their long exile has been part of the refining process by which God is making them ready for restoration. That is why God makes a special distinction between Israel and all other nations:

"Then fear not, O Jacob my servant," declares the LORD,
"nor be dismayed, O Israel; for behold, I will save you from far away, and your offspring from the land of their captivity. Jacob shall return and have quiet and ease, and none shall make him afraid. For I am with you to save you," declares the LORD;
"I will make a full end of all the nations among whom I scattered you, but of you I will not make a full end. I will

> **discipline you in just measure, and I will by no means leave
> you unpunished.**"
> —Jeremiah 30:10-11 (emphasis added)

This is why Paul could state with confidence when questioned by both Jewish and Roman authorities, "And now I stand here on trial because of my hope in the promise made by God to our fathers, to which our twelve tribes hope to attain, as they earnestly worship night and day" (Acts 26:6-7). It is also why Paul could exhort the Gentile followers of Jesus in Rome to be respectful and inclusive of their Jewish brethren, concluding his instruction with these words:

> Lest you be wise in your own sight, I do not want you to
> be unaware of this mystery, brothers: a partial hardening
> has come upon Israel, until the fullness of the Gentiles has
> come in. **And in this way all Israel will be saved,** as it is
> written, "The Deliverer will come from Zion, he will banish
> ungodliness from Jacob"; "and this will be my covenant with
> them when I take away their sins." As regards the gospel, they
> are enemies for your sake. **But as regards election, they are
> beloved for the sake of their forefathers. For the gifts and
> the calling of God are irrevocable.**
> —Romans 11:25-29 (emphasis added)

We could go on to investigate John's vision in the book of Revelation of a restored Israel in the New Jerusalem—not in heaven, but in that same Promised Land on the eastern shore of the Mediterranean Sea. That land will be populated by the native-born of Israel, as well as the foreigners who have joined them, and they will enter the city through the twelve gates named for Israel's twelve tribes (Revelation 7:1-17, 21:9-

14; see also Ezekiel 47:13-22, 48:30-35). That is consistent with Jesus' promise to his disciples that they would judge the twelve tribes of Israel (Matthew 19:28).

What should be clear is this: *the promises of God are eternal and irrevocable.* He has staked his very name and reputation on his willingness and ability to come through on his promises. If God doesn't come through on his promises to the Jewish people, can we trust him to come through on any promises?

CHAPTER 5

BECAUSE OF THE HISTORICAL RECORD

We study history to find out what is important in our shared human experience. What people observed in ages past and how they interpreted it reveal what mattered most to them in their time. If we, in our time, observe the same aspects of life and also consider them important, then it is likely that those shared aspects are among the constant factors that shape our human experience and define who we are.

The constants that readily come to mind include love, marriage, family, moral definitions of right and wrong, quality of life, and the inevitability of death. These qualities transcend cultures, ethnicities, and religions. That should not be surprising. It *is* surprising, however, when we find not only enduring qualities but also a particular *people group* as a constant feature of our human experience. It is already remarkable when a people survives for millennia, and even more remarkable if they have a continuous impact on human civilization, even in the face of unrelenting opposition. If such a people exists, then perhaps we could learn something from them about why all of humanity exists, and perhaps even what our Creator considers important.

Such a people does exist. They are the Jewish people of God's Covenant Nation of Israel. Mark Twain, the famous American novelist of the 19th century, wrote about them in a thought-provoking essay in 1899. The rampant antisemitism in Europe in those days prompted him to write about the condition of the Jewish people throughout history. He noted that the anti-Jewish sentiment of his day was nothing new, but in fact is a constant feature of the human story. The Jews had not invited such universal hatred, nor done anything to deserve it. However, it was there just the same as it had been in ancient Egypt. In his conclusion, Twain left us with a question:

> If the statistics are right, the Jews constitute but *one per cent* of the human race. It suggests a nebulous dim puff of star dust lost in the blaze of the Milky Way. Properly the Jew ought hardly to be heard of; but he is heard of, has always been heard of. He is as prominent on the planet as any other people, and his commercial importance is extravagantly out of proportion to the smallness of his bulk. His contributions to the world's list of great names in literature, science, art, music, finance, medicine, and abstruse learning are also away out of proportion to the weakness of his numbers. He has made a marvelous fight in this world, in all the ages; and has done it with his hands tied behind him. He could be vain of himself, and be excused for it. The Egyptian, the Babylonian, and the Persian rose, filled the planet with sound and splendor, then faded to dream-stuff and passed away; the Greek and Roman followed, and made a vast noise, and they are gone; other peoples have sprung up and held their torch high for a time, but it burned out, and they sit in twilight now, or have vanished. The Jew saw them all, beat them all, and is now what he always was, exhibiting no decadence, no infirmities of age, no weakening of his parts, no slowing of his energies, no dulling of his alert and aggressive mind. All things are mortal but the Jew; all other forces pass, but he remains. What is the secret of his immortality?[1]

---

1   Mark Twain, "Concerning the Jews," *Harper's New Monthly Magazine* 99 No. 589 (June 1899): 527-535, https://archive.org/details/harpersmagazine99junalde/page/n5/

Mark Twain was not known to be very religious, but if pressed to answer his own question, he might have said that the secret to the immortality of the Jewish people lies in their being chosen by God. That is what God told Moses to tell the people of Israel at Mount Sinai, just before he gave them the Ten Commandments:

> "Thus you shall say to the house of Jacob, and tell the people of Israel: 'You yourselves have seen what I did to the Egyptians, and how I bore you on eagles' wings and brought you to myself. **Now therefore, if you will indeed obey my voice and keep my covenant, you shall be my treasured possession among all peoples,** for all the earth is mine; and you shall be to me a kingdom of priests and a holy nation.' These are the words that you shall speak to the people of Israel."
> —Exodus 19:3-6 (emphasis added)

God reiterated this several times (Deuteronomy 7:6; 14:2; 26:18). Keeping his commandments would be a feature of his people's special status among the nations, but Israel's record on that count was spotty at best. God knew that would be the case even as he created the nation. Their obedience, or lack thereof, would not disqualify them from being his chosen people. He had made that decision long before he brought them out of Egypt. To use a New Testament term, the nation of Israel was predestined to be God's chosen people for a specific reason:

> For you are a people holy to the LORD your God. **The LORD your God has chosen you to be a people for his treasured possession, out of all the peoples who are on the face of the**

mode/2up.

earth. It was not because you were more in number than any other people that the LORD set his love on you and chose you, for you were the fewest of all peoples, but **it is because the LORD loves you and is keeping the oath that he swore to your fathers**, that the LORD has brought you out with a mighty hand and redeemed you from the house of slavery, from the hand of Pharaoh king of Egypt.
—Deuteronomy 7:6-8 (emphasis added)

It comes down to this: God is proving to everyone in heaven and on earth and under the earth that he will have his way, no matter what obstacles are in his path. He intends to redeem this earth, and his vehicle of redemption is the Covenant Nation he called into existence through Abraham. That is a big part of the meaning behind God's promise to Abraham and his descendants that through them all the nations of the earth would be blessed (Genesis 18:17-19, 22:15-18, 26:3-5, 28:10-15). The strength of the Covenant depends not on the obedience of the Chosen People, but on the grace and faithfulness of the One who made the Covenant, as the writer of Hebrews reminds us:

For when God made a promise to Abraham, since he had no one greater by whom to swear, he swore by himself, saying, "Surely I will bless you and multiply you."
—Hebrews 6:13 (cf. Genesis 22:16-18)

This is why the Jewish people have survived as a people and as the visible remnant of the nation of Israel for nearly 4,000 years. The book of Genesis records the providence of God in preserving his people even before they were a people. In Abraham's day, they were known as Hebrews, the people who had come from across the river Euphrates. It would be many years before Abraham's grandson, Jacob, would acquire the name of Israel, and another generation before Jacob's son, Judah, imparted the name Yehudi (Jew) to the tribe, house, and kingdom he fathered.

In the early days, God intervened miraculously to deal with the barrenness of the Patriarchs' wives, ensuring that Sarah, Rebekah, and Rachel bore children to Abraham, Isaac, and Jacob, respectively. Leah, Rachel's sister and Jacob's first wife, suffered a different kind of barrenness in that Jacob loved her sister more even though she had born him six sons and a daughter. God addressed that as well, providing comfort and healing to a family in need of both. His hand is evident in such events, but do we also recognize his presence in less miraculous ways, as he guided the family through other challenges? Consider these examples:

- Attempts by the Pharaoh of Egypt and the king of the Philistines to take Sarah and Rebekah into their harems (Genesis 12:10-20, 20:1-18, 26:6-16).
- Efforts of the Canaanite peoples to intermarry with and assimilate the family into their own cultures (Genesis 26:34, 34:1-31, 38:1-30).
- Schemes of Laban the Syrian to keep Jacob and his family in bondage to him perpetually (Genesis 29:1-30, 31:1-55).
- Rivalry of Jacob's wives, Leah and Rachel, in which Leah felt unloved even though she had born Jacob six sons and a daughter (Genesis 29:30-30:21).
- Plans of Esau to murder his brother Jacob and acquire the birthright by force (Genesis 27:41-28:5, 32:3-21, 33:1-17).
- Contention over ownership of the land and its resources (Genesis 21:22-34, 26:6-33).

These threats occurred even though the Hebrews were good neighbors who sought to live at peace with the people of the land and even allied with them in a war to liberate Canaan from foreign invaders (Genesis 14:1-24). Through it all, the Hebrews dwelt as a small minority in a land not yet their own and somehow managed to prosper. In the transition from Genesis to Exodus, we see that the family consisted of only 70 people, but they were very wealthy (Exodus 1:1-7). Their wealth and status in Egypt caused the Egyptians to resent and fear them, leading to their enslavement and attempted genocide by the Pharaohs. God intervened, preserving and multiplying the people even in their trials. When he brought them out of Egypt with a mighty hand, many Egyptians and others came with them, swelling the numbers of the Covenant Nation to over 600,000 men of military age and their families (Exodus 12:37-38).

It took 40 years of wandering in the wilderness before the Israelites entered and conquered the Promised Land, then 400 years under the Judges before Saul became Israel's first king. David and Solomon followed Saul, but after only 120 years of a united kingdom, Israel split into two rival states. The Assyrian Empire conquered the northern kingdom of Israel about 200 years later, and 140 years after that, the Babylonians conquered the southern kingdom of Judah.

This is where the continued existence of Israel becomes interesting. With no homeland as the center of an independent state, the survival of the Jewish people was in doubt. By the time the Babylonians destroyed Jerusalem and the Temple in 586 BC, the northern kingdom had been dispersed for over three generations. Those tribes continued to wander, eventually assimilating with many nations and losing their identity as Hebrews. There are prophecies of their return, and Jewish efforts to find the Lost Tribes continue to this day. As of now, however, the people of Israel's northern kingdom remain assimilated among the nations.

Why did that not happen to the Jewish people? Why did they remain a distinct people, holding tightly to the Torah[2] and their identity as Israelites?

The obvious answer is that they really are God's Chosen People, custodians of his Covenant of redemption (Romans 9:4-5). That is an answer the world would rather not hear, because admitting that the Jews have survived because of God's continued intervention on their behalf means admitting that there really is a God who one day will call every nation and person to account. Moreover, it means admitting that the Jews have a key role to play in God's plans. That is where it gets uncomfortable even for those who profess faith in the God of Abraham, Isaac, and Jacob. The persistent survival of observant Jews who remain faithful to the Torah hints that God's ways just might have something to do with what Moses taught. That, by the way, is what Jesus tells us (Matthew 5:17-20, 23:2; John 5:45-47).

This is why the historical record is so important. It's easy to spiritualize the Bible and relegate the Jews to its ancient texts, but we can't do that when the Jews continue to exist as Jews, especially when they return to their land as God promised. What we should do is rejoice in our God who comes through on his promises by preserving his Chosen People through the ages.

---

2   The Torah, often called the Law, or the Law of Moses, contains the law, teaching, and commandments of God as written in the five books of Moses (Genesis, Exodus, Leviticus, Numbers, Deuteronomy). Jewish reverence for the Torah extends as well to the voluminous commentaries on the scriptures recorded in the Mishnah and Gemara, which together comprise the Talmud. Both versions of the Talmud (Babylonian and Jerusalem) are available digitally at https://www.sefaria.org/texts/Talmud.

We learn from the Bible that God guided the Jewish people through the captivity in Babylon, and opened the way for their return to the land of Israel after 70 years (605-537 BC; see the Book of Daniel). When the Persian Empire conquered Babylon, God advocated for his people in the resettlement of Judea and the rebuilding of Jerusalem (see Ezra and Nehemiah). In that same era, God saved the Jewish people from genocide during the reign of Xerxes I (486-465 BC) and his viceroy, Haman (see Esther). After Persia fell to the Greeks under Alexander the Great, the main threat to the Jewish people was assimilation, but God preserved a faithful remnant. That remnant remained true to him when the threat of assimilation became yet another threat of genocide during the reign of Antiochus IV Epiphanes (175-164 BC). The books of Maccabees tell us how God worked through the faithful remnant to defeat the Greeks and restore worship of God in the Temple.

As the centuries passed into the present era, the Jewish people came under the power of the Roman Empire. Rome's client, Herod the Great, spilled much Jewish blood in his grandiose building projects and paranoia over threats to his reign, but the fact that he and his descendants were personal friends of the Caesars often worked in the favor of the Jews. That was the climate in which Jesus of Nazareth was born and what became the Christian church came into existence.

Christians are familiar with the schemes of certain Jewish leaders to eliminate Jesus because of the threat he posed to their power, but many are less familiar with the efforts of God to preserve the Jewish people even though their leaders chose to condemn Jesus. In Christian eyes, that was the greatest infraction of the era, but it was actually a symptom of a systemic issue that brought about the destruction of the second Temple and a second exile of the Jewish people. According to Jewish sources, those disasters were the divine response to baseless, or wanton, hatred:

However, considering that the people during the Second
Temple period were engaged in Torah study, observance of
mitzvot [commandments], and acts of kindness, and that they
did not perform the sinful acts that were performed in the
First Temple, why was the Second Temple destroyed? It was
destroyed due to the fact that there was wanton hatred during
that period. This comes to teach you that the sin of wanton
hatred is equivalent to the three severe transgressions: Idol
worship, forbidden sexual relations and bloodshed.[3]

The crucifixion of Jesus and the subsequent persecution of his followers was but one example of this baseless hatred. Jewish society at the
time was so divided that factions fought against one another even as
Rome's legions besieged Jerusalem during the Great Jewish War (66-73
AD).[4] The disastrous loss to the Romans, culminating in the siege of
Masada, was but the beginning of sorrows. In the year 132, in a final,
desperate effort to overthrow Roman occupation, Simon Bar Kohkba
raised an ill-fated revolt that bears his name. When the Romans put
down the uprising three years later, Emperor Hadrian decreed that
Judea would be renamed Syria-Palaestina (later shortened to Palestine).
Jerusalem became a pagan city called Aelia Capitolina, and Jews were
forbidden from entering the city except on the 9th of Av, the day of
mourning commemorating the destruction of both Temples.[5]

---

3   Babylonian Talmud, Yoma 9b, *The William Davidson digital edition of the Koren Noé
     Talmud*, https://www.sefaria.org/Yoma.9b.8?lang=bi&with=About&lang2=en.

4   Joseph Telushkin, "The Great Revolt (66-70 CE)," *Jewish Virtual Library*, reprinted by
     permission from Joseph Telushkin, *Jewish Literacy: The Most Important Things to Know
     About the Jewish Religion, Its People and Its History* (New York: William Morrow and Co.,
     1991), https://www.jewishvirtuallibrary.org/the-great-revolt-66-70-ce.

5   "The Bar-Kokhba Revolt (132-135 CE)," *Jewish Virtual Library*, https://www.

The two wars against Rome cost the lives of a million Jewish people and the exile of many more. Roman persecution of the Jews escalated, with decrees forbidding Torah study, Sabbath observance, and circumcision. Having lost their Temple, their homeland, their centers of learning, and much more, the Jewish nation was in danger of extinction. Jews lived precariously in the years between the end of the Bar Kokhba Revolt in 135 and the First Aliyah (return to the land) in 1882. They were scattered literally to every nation on earth, always as outcasts and foreigners and often under suspicion as threats to the nations where they sojourned. In Christian lands, Jews were reviled as "Christ killers" and easy targets for angry mobs eager to find scapegoats for their misfortunes. After Islam came on the scene in the year 622, Jews along with Christians and other non-Muslims, were relegated to subservience in Muslim lands, subjected to special taxes, social restrictions, and enslavement. Even so, Jewish communities managed to find safe spaces and thrive, although their security always depended on the goodwill of their Christian and Muslim neighbors, and that could change in an instant.

The massacres of Jewish communities in Germany's Rhineland at the start of the First Crusade in 1096 marked a turning point in Jewish history. The Crusade was launched with the aim of liberating Jerusalem and the Holy Land from Muslim occupation, but the first targets were the Jews of France and Germany. In the spring of 1096, anti-Jewish violence inspired by the Crusade took the lives of one-quarter of the Jewish population of Germany and northern France, 12,000 of them in the Rhine Valley.[6] An entire German school of Torah commentary was completely eradicated. The loss to Jewish learning, culture, and

---

jewishvirtuallibrary.org/the-bar-kokhba-revolt-132-135-ce.

6   O'Dell and Montgomery, *The LIST*, 130-131.

community life was immeasurable and made even more bitter by the unexpected nature of the Crusaders' assaults. As one modern Jewish scholar explains:

> Dr. Haym Soloveitchik once noted that the Crusades represented the last time Jews of Ashkenaz (writ large) [Jews who settled in Central and Eastern Europe] were surprised by their persecution. Following the Crusades, Jewish history in Ashkenaz (as described by a famous Jewish historian) was written in blood rather than in ink. We went from persecution to persecution, from blood libel to allegations of well-poisoning and host desecration, from pogrom to pogrom. Our lives were constantly at ill-ease. We never felt secure. Promises made by kings and governors almost always rang completely hollow. The Crusades may represent the first time since Churban HaBayit [destruction of the Temple] when Jews were surprised by an attack. It was this feeling of surprise, this sudden loss of security, that may be why the Crusades continue to occupy such a major place in our consciousness.[7]

The First Crusade marked an escalation of Christian hostility to Jewish communities. Blood libels—accusations that Jews murdered Christians to use their blood in religious rituals—periodically inspired new rounds of anti-Jewish violence, as in Norwich, England, in 1144, and again in Lincoln in 1255. When the presence of Jews became too obnoxious, magistrates and kings would order them expelled, as did

---

7   Rabbi Ezra Schwartz, "The Kinnot of the Crusades," Rabbi Isaac Elchanan Theological Seminary, Yeshiva University, New York, July 21, 2018, https://www.yutorah.org/lectures/911405.

King Edward I of England in 1290, and King Phillip IV of France in 1306.[8]

The Black Death (Bubonic plague) that took the lives of 25 million Europeans from 1348-51 brought more reason to target Jews. Rumors abounded that Jews had concocted the plague to kill Christians, allegedly carrying out the plan through means like poisoning wells. Riots broke out in communities across the continent, taking the lives of thousands of innocent Jews. In some of the worst instances, 600 Jews were burned alive in Basel, Switzerland in January 1349, and 6,000 in Mainz, Germany, in August of the same year.[9]

Perhaps the greatest systematic persecution of Jews began in Spain in 1478, when King Ferdinand and Queen Isabella partnered with the Catholic Church to launch the Inquisition. Any person suspected of departing from the official doctrines of the church could be arrested, tried, and executed, often by burning at the stake. Suspects included Christian heretics, as well as Muslims and Jews. In 1492, Ferdinand and Isabella decreed that all Muslims and Jews who refused to convert would be expelled from Spain by July 31. Up to 300,000 chose to leave in what became the largest deportation of Jews before the Holocaust. Many fled to Muslim countries in North Africa, while others chose to return to the land of Israel. It is no coincidence that Christopher Columbus, who sympathized with the Jews and may even have been Jewish, chose to depart on his famous voyage of discovery on the day before the expulsion decree took effect.[10]

Many Spanish and Portuguese Jews chose to convert to Christianity, at least nominally. These conversos often continued to practice

---

8   O'Dell and Montgomery, *The LIST*, 140, 178, 194, 200.
9   Ibid, 205-214.
10   Ibid, 251-258.

Judaism in secret, at peril of their lives. As Spain became a global empire, conversos and other Jews sought refuge in the colonies, where they could more easily hide their identity from the prying eyes of the Inquisition. To this day, many "hidden Jews," or *Anusim*, in the United States, Mexico, and Central and South America are awakening to their Jewish identity.[11]

As the Protestant Reformation took shape in the 16th century, leaders like Martin Luther and John Calvin took issue with many corrupt and biblically questionable practices of the Catholic Church. Although Luther initially took a more conciliatory position regarding the Jewish people, noting that Jesus was a Jew, he eventually adopted a very harsh tone when the Jews he encountered refused to accept the Protestant gospel he preached. In 1543, he published two essays, "On the Jews and their Lies" and "Of the Unknowable Name and the Generations of Christ," in which he condemned the Jews for rejecting Christ, charging that they were no longer God's Chosen People but had become "the devil's children." Luther's writings outlined a program of repression against Jewish communities and religious practices that inspired the Nazi anti-Jewish propaganda and justification of the Holocaust.[12]

Luther's antisemitism was not unique among Protestants. Disdain of the Jews had become ingrained in Christian culture for 1,500 years, and could not easily be removed. Jews remained pariahs in popular culture, as evident in works such as Chaucer's *The Canterbury Tales*

---

11   Revis Daggett, "The Shadow of the Inquisition," interview by Albert J. McCarn, *Reunion Roadmap Israel Connections*, October 27, 2024, audio, https://www.buzzsprout.com/2292194/episodes/15678974.

12   O'Dell and Montgomery, *The LIST*, 273-276, 278-280, 284-289.

and Shakespeare's *The Merchant of Venice*. Nevertheless, they not only survived, but prospered spiritually, intellectually, and even financially.

The Judaism we know today was shaped by sages such as Rabbi Akiva ben Joseph (c. 50-135), Rabbi Shlomo Yitzchaki (Rashi) (1040-1105), Rabbi Moses ben Maimon (Rambam, or Maimonides) (1138-1204), Rabbi Moses ben Nachman (Ramban, or Nachmanides) (1194-1270), and Rabbi Elijah ben Solomon Zalman (the Vilna Gaon) (1720-1797). These scholars wrestled with application of the Torah in the exile, while never losing faith in the God who had promised to restore Israel and usher in the Messianic Age. Their wisdom and knowledge influenced Christian and Muslim learning as well. Some even took positions of great influence, such as Maimonides, who became the court physician to Sultan Saladin, the man who defeated the Crusaders and recaptured Jerusalem in 1187.

Jews became influential in other areas as well. The philosopher Baruch de Spinoza (1632-1677) became an early proponent of rationalism and a forerunner of the Age of Enlightenment. Haym Salomon (1740-1785), a Polish-born Jewish merchant, became known as the financier of the American Revolution and was one of many prominent Jews who contributed to the American cause.

Perhaps the most influential Jewish financiers were, and are, the Rothschild family. Mayer Amschel Rothschild (1744-1812) of Frankfurt, Germany, was an innovator in international finance. He divided his fortune among his sons, who then established banking families in Austria, England, Naples, and France. Those families became intertwined with the nobility of their host nations and financed much of the industrialization of Europe and the world.

Much has been written about the Rothschilds. Conspiracy theorists are quick to include them among the ultra-rich ancient bloodlines that supposedly have determined the fate of the world. It is true that the Rothschild families have profited over the centuries by financing wars—even lending to opposing sides. Their wealth and influence continue to cause suspicion and resentment, and the fact that they are Jewish compounds that negative sentiment. That, however, does not mean the whole family is satanically inspired, but rather that they are shrewd at business and just as prone as anyone to engage in unethical practices. Thus, it is even more remarkable that God used the Rothschild family to shepherd the rebirth of the nation of Israel.

The Rothschild connection to Israel's rebirth is personified in the work of two prominent members of the family: Baron Edmond de Rothschild of France (1845-1934) and Walter Rothschild, second Baron Rothschild of England (1868-1937). Both became interested in the Zionist cause at its inception.

As the rise of antisemitism in the late 19th century inspired many Jews to seek refuge outside Europe, the Zionist movement developed with the idea that the Jewish people should return to their ancient ancestral home in Eretz Israel (the land of Israel). There were considerable obstacles to that dream, not the least being that Israel, or Palestine as it was still called, was part of the Turkish Ottoman Empire. The Ottoman Sultans had little interest in catering to Jewish petitioners, and the rest of the Great Powers (Great Britain, France, Russia, Germany, Austria-Hungary, Italy, and the United States) had little interest in changing the status quo in the Middle East. Creating a Jewish homeland would mean either receiving special dispensation from the Turks for a Jewish province, or the dismemberment of the Ottoman Empire and the creation of a power vacuum in the Middle East and Southeastern Europe. On top of that, Palestine was a desolate, largely uninhabited backwater, infested with swamps, deserts, and barren wastes. Where would the returning Jews find places to live, and how would they make their living?

That was where the Great Benefactor, Baron Edmond de Rothschild, stepped in. The first Jewish returnees began to arrive from Europe and Yemen in 1882 in what is called the First Aliyah. From that year through 1903, 35,000 Jews came to Palestine, many of whom subsequently returned to Europe. Those who remained were able to do so largely because of the philanthropy of Baron de Rothschild, who financed the new communities of Rishon Lezion, Rosh Pina, and Zichron Ya'akov. He also provided agricultural and other advisors to assist the pioneers and purchased many tracts of land from Arab and Turkish landowners that would be turned into productive farms, vineyards, and villages.[13]

As Edmond de Rothschild was financing the return of Jewish pioneers, his relative, Baron Walter Rothschild, used his influence as a member of Parliament to sway the government in favor of the Zionist cause. He entered Parliament in 1899, just two years after the World Zionist Organization was established at the First Zionist Congress in Basel, Switzerland.

The Congress itself was something of a miracle. Theodor Herzl, a Hungarian-born Jewish lawyer and journalist, convened the Congress as a practical first step toward addressing the problem of antisemitism. As a journalist, he had covered the trial of Alfred Dreyfus, a French army officer falsely accused of spying for Germany. The proceedings against the Jewish Dreyfus incited vitriolic hatred against Jews from all elements of French society, which in turn convinced Herzl that there was no solution to the Jewish problem other than providing a homeland

---

13 "Immigration to Israel: The First Aliyah (1882 - 1903)," *Jewish Virtual Library*, https://www.jewishvirtuallibrary.org/the-first-aliyah-1882-1903; "Baron Edmond De Rothschild (1845 - 1934)," *Jewish Virtual Library*, https://www.jewishvirtuallibrary.org/baron-edmond-de-rothschild.

for the Jews outside Europe. He published his thoughts on the matter in a short book called *Der Judenstaat* (The Jewish State) in 1896,[14] and in 1897 had enough support to convene the First Zionist Congress, which adopted as its program the establishment of "a home for the Jewish people in Eretz-Israel secured under public law." It is instructive to review the means by which the Zionist Congress intended to achieve this goal:

1. The promotion by appropriate means of the settlement in Eretz-Israel of Jewish farmers, artisans, and manufacturers.
2. The organization and uniting of the whole of Jewry by means of appropriate institutions, both local and international, in accordance with the laws of each country.
3. The strengthening and fostering of Jewish national sentiment and national consciousness.
4. Preparatory steps toward obtaining the consent of governments, where necessary, in order to reach the goals of Zionism.[15]

The Basel Program, as the Zionist agenda came to be known, was far more ambitious than settling Jews in their ancient homeland. The educational, financial, institutional, diplomatic, and communal aspects of the program aimed at nothing less than the resurrection of the nation of Israel, just as Ezekiel envisioned in his prophecy of the Dry

---

14 A digital edition of *Der Judenstaat* is available in English through Project Gutenberg at https://www.gutenberg.org/files/25282/25282-h/25282-h.htm. This edition, originally published in 1946 by the American Zionist Emergency Council, New York, contains significant background information on the antisemitism of the era in the Introduction by Louis Lipsky, and a biography of Theodor Herzl based on the work of Alex Bein.

15 "First Zionist Congress & Basel Program (August 1897)," *Jewish Virtual Library*, https://www.jewishvirtuallibrary.org/first-zionist-congress-and-basel-program-1897.

Bones (Ezekiel 37:1-14). It is ironic that many, if not most, of those who took part in the Zionist program, including Herzl, were secular Jews. There was a significant presence of observant Jews, especially those from Russia and Eastern Europe, but many embraced Zionism as the logical nationalistic expression of the Jewish people, just as the Greek, Romanian, Hungarian, and other peoples were expressing their nationalistic aspirations for their homelands. When we add to the mix the Marxist views of many of the early Zionists, we should be even more amazed at who God uses for his purposes.

Herzl devoted the rest of his life to the Zionist cause, exhausting both his health and his family's fortune in traveling across Europe and the Middle East to meet heads of state and other dignitaries who could act on behalf of the Jewish dream. He was helped in this work by Reverend William Hechler, an Anglican priest who used his connections as chaplain of the British Embassy in Vienna to open doors for Herzl. Hechler's favorable views toward Zionism were an expression of a growing pro-Jewish sentiment among Christians who had begun to take notice of God's promises to restore Israel. That in itself is another indication of God's provision for his Chosen People.[16]

By the time of Herzl's death in 1904, Zionism had become a movement that simultaneously united and divided Jewish communities. Those who suffered through the pogroms (anti-Jewish riots) in the east, such as the one in Kishinev, Moldova in 1903, that took the lives of 49 Jews, embraced Zionism as the means to escape escalating persecution and enable them to walk fully into their identity as Jews. Those

---

16 Phillip Earl Steele, "British Christian Zionism (Part 3): Reverend William Hechler – from Hovevei Zion to Herzl and beyond," *Fathom*, April 2022, https://fathomjournal. org/british-christian-zionism-part-3-reverend-william-hechler-from-hovevei-zion-to-herzl-and-beyond/.

who lived in Western Europe and America, where antisemitism was a constant, but tolerable, feature of life, were more inclined to assimilate into their host societies and oppose Zionism as a threat to their security. That was nothing new; in ancient times, Jewish communities were similarly divided between those who advocated assimilation and those who took a stand for remaining true to their Hebrew identity, to the Torah, and to the God of Israel.[17]

World War I changed the landscape, not only for Zionism, but for the global world order. The world entered the war in 1914 divided among the interests of the Great Powers. After its conclusion in 1918, the subsequent peace settlements dismembered four of those Powers. Civil war raged in Russia as the Tsarist Empire was transformed into the communist Union of Soviet Socialist Republics (USSR). Austria-Hungary dissolved into independent nationalist states based on ethnic majorities. Germany's empire was also dismembered, both in Europe and overseas, and the Ottoman Empire was reduced to the borders of present-day Turkey.

The collapse of the Ottoman Empire, which the other Powers had spent nearly two centuries trying to prevent, was finally brought about by the massive war that no one wanted. In expectation that the Turkish possessions would be diminished, Great Britain and France collaborated on plans to fill the inevitable power vacuum by dividing up the Middle East between themselves. Under the Sykes-Picot

---

17 This theme of assimilation vs. faithfulness to the Torah is evident in the books of Ezra, Nehemiah, and Esther, as well as the story of the Maccabees. It was also present in Egypt at the time of the Exodus. One line of Jewish thought is that only one-fifth of the Hebrews left with Moses. The other four-fifths died in Egypt during the plague of darkness because they had become assimilated and would not leave ("How Many Israelites Died in the Plague of Darkness?," *The Israel Bible*, January 6, 2022, https://theisraelbible.com/how-many-israelites-died-when-the-lights-went-out-in-egypt/.)

Agreement of March 1916, the two Western empires agreed to extend their control over neighboring spheres of influence in the Middle East. Developments during and after the war caused considerable modification to the agreement, but eventually, under the newly established League of Nations, Britain received a mandate over Iraq and Palestine (at that time, including all of Israel and Jordan), while France received a mandate over Syria and Lebanon (see Map 6, British Mandate for Palestine). The mandatory powers were charged with creating the conditions for national self-determination of the peoples under their control, eventually resulting in independent Arab and Jewish states.[18]

At the same time, other elements of the British government and military collaborated with Arab and Jewish partners, promising states of their own in return for help against the Turks. The legendary Lawrence of Arabia, Colonel T.E. Lawrence, led the effort to enlist the aid of Arab tribes, resulting in creation of an Arab army under Sherif Feisal ibn Hussein that carried the war from the Arabian Peninsula to Damascus.[19] On the Jewish side, Vladimir Jabotinsky, a Russian-born journalist and Zionist advocate, proposed the enlistment of a Jewish Legion of volunteers to serve in the British Army. With help from Chaim Weizmann, another Russian-born Zionist with significant political connections in Britain, among others, Jabotinsky's idea soon became reality, and the Jewish Legion was formed with volunteers from

---

18 Scott Christianson and Chris Heller, "The Origins of the World War I Agreement That Carved Up the Middle East: How Great Britain and France secretly negotiated the Sykes-Picot Agreement," *Smithsonian Magazine*, November 16, 2015, https://www.smithsonianmag.com/history/sykes-picot-agreement-180957217/; "The League of Nations," *United Nations Office at Geneva*, https://www.ungeneva.org/en/about/league-of-nations/overview.

19 "Who Was Lawrence of Arabia?" *Imperial War Museum*, London, https://www.iwm.org.uk/history/who-was-lawrence-of-arabia.

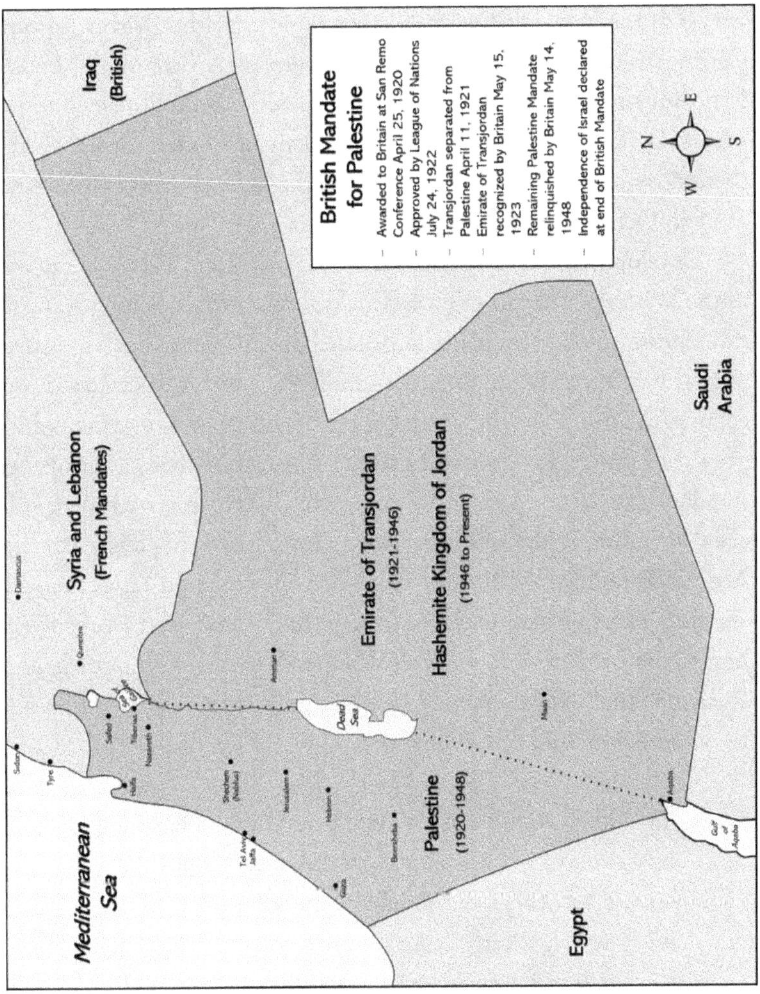

Map 6. British Mandate for Palestine. (Based on Public Domain map by Zero0000, via Wikimedia Commons, https://commons.wikimedia.org/wiki/File:BritishMandatePalestine1920.svg.)

Jewish Palestinian refugees and other Jews from the British Empire, Canada, and the United States. The Legion was part of the British Expeditionary Force under Field Marshall Edmund Allenby that advanced from Egypt to liberate Jerusalem in December 1917, and then move on to Damascus, arriving at the same time as Feisal's Arab army in October 1918.[20]

Developments on the battlefields of Arabia and Palestine, as well as the Western Front in France, provided opportunities for advancing the Zionist cause, particularly in Britain. Chaim Weizmann was instrumental in this regard. As an accomplished chemist, he developed procedures to streamline the production of artillery ammunition, which proved of immense importance to the Allied war effort. That opened the door for his connection to a number of British government officials, including Prime Minister David Lloyd George, Foreign Minister Arthur Balfour, and Minister of Munitions Winston Churchill. He was also a close friend of Baron Walter Rothschild, and worked with him to draft a declaration of British support for a Jewish homeland in Palestine. Their efforts resulted in the famous letter from Lord Balfour to Baron Rothschild of November 2, 1917, which declared:

> His Majesty's Government view with favour the establishment in Palestine of a national home for the Jewish people, and will use their best endeavors to facilitate the achievement of this object, it being clearly understood that nothing shall be done which may prejudice the civil and religious rights of existing

---

20 Jewish Legion, *Jewish Virtual Library*, https://www.jewishvirtuallibrary.org/jewish-legion.

non-Jewish communities in Palestine or the rights and political status enjoyed by Jews in any other country.[21]

The Balfour Declaration was a major milestone in the return of God's Chosen People to the Promised Land, but it was not the end of the process. If anything, it was the beginning of the next phase of God's millennia-long project with his Covenant Nation. Jews had become established in Eretz Israel, building flourishing communities and reviving the ancient Hebrew language, but they still faced tremendous opposition, starting with the competing claims to the land based on the conflicting commitments Britain had made during the war. By the mid-1920s, the British had navigated the postwar settlements somewhat successfully by placing Feisal on the throne of the newly created kingdom of Iraq, and his brother Abdullah on the throne of the newly created kingdom of Jordan on the eastern side of the Jordan River. The French had taken control over Syria and Lebanon, and the remaining territory in Palestine west of the Jordan was to have become the long-awaited Jewish state.

It was at that point that British support for the Zionist cause wavered in the face of Arab agitation. The leader of the anti-Jewish efforts was Hajj Amin al-Husayni, a Jerusalem-born cleric whom the British appointed Grand Mufti of Jerusalem in 1921. The incitement he sponsored set the pattern for continued opposition to Jewish presence in the Holy Land to this day, adopting tactics such as demonstrations, civil disobedience, terrorism, riots, and mass murder. Al-Husayni justified these actions by claiming that Jewish presence in Palestine was

21   "Chaim Weizmann," The National Library of Israel, https://www.nli.org.il/en/discover/israel/figures/chaim-weizmann; "Balfour Declaration: Text of the Declaration," Jewish Virtual Library, https://www.jewishvirtuallibrary.org/text-of-the-balfour-declaration.

an existential threat to Islam, especially because of the alleged Jewish intent to remove the Al Aqsa Mosque and rebuild the Temple in Jerusalem. In 1929, the Mufti's incitement led to riots throughout Palestine, including the massacre of 67 Jews in the community of Hebron. As a result, the British evacuated the entire Jewish community, leaving Hebron, the city of the Patriarchs, without a Jewish presence for the first time in millennia.[22]

Arab violence escalated in the 1930s, leading the British in 1937 to propose dividing the land into Jewish and Arab zones, leading to two states. This proposal, named for the Peel Commission that developed it, was the first of many partition plans that could have led to independent Arab and Jewish states living in peace alongside one another (see Map 7, Peel Commission Proposal for Partition of Palestine, 1937).

Both the Jews and the Arabs rejected the Peel Commission proposal. The Jews were open to sharing the land, but the Arabs were not. Palestinian Arabs have rejected every offer of a two-state solution since 1937.[23]

In the face of an open Arab revolt and a growing threat from Adolf Hitler's Germany, the British adopted a conciliatory tone with the Arabs, although they took measures to suppress the revolt. The Mufti fled to Lebanon before the British could detain him for his role in

---

22   "Hajj Amin al-Husayni: The Mufti of Jerusalem," *Holocaust Encyclopedia*, United States Holocaust Memorial Museum, https://encyclopedia.ushmm.org/content/en/article/hajj-amin-al-husayni-the-mufti-of-jerusalem; Hajj Amin al-Husayni: Arab Nationalist and Muslim Leader, ibid. https://encyclopedia.ushmm.org/content/en/article/hajj-amin-al-husayni-arab-nationalist-and-muslim-leader?parent=en%2F11094; "Hebron: History and Overview," *Jewish Virtual Library*, https://www.jewishvirtuallibrary.org/history-and-overview-of-hebron.

23   "The Peel Commission Plan (1937)," Israel Ministry of Foreign Affairs, https://embassies. gov.il/MFA/AboutIsrael/Maps/Pages/The-Peel-Commission-Plan-1937.aspx.

the uprising and in time made his way to Europe, where he became a collaborator with Hitler and the Nazi leaders.

In the spring of 1939, the British government of Prime Minister Neville Chamberlain (the same man who sought to secure "peace in our time" by handing Czechoslovakia over to Hitler) outlined a new policy for British Mandatory Palestine. As articulated in the infamous White Paper, this policy stated:

> His Majesty's Government therefore now declare unequiv-
> ocally that it is not part of their policy that Palestine should
> become a Jewish State. They would indeed regard it as contrary
> to their obligations to the Arabs under the Mandate, as well as
> to the assurances which have been given to the Arab people in
> the past, that the Arab population of Palestine should be made
> the subjects of a Jewish State against their will.[24]

The White Paper went on to outline steps toward the establishment of an integrated Arab-Jewish state over the next ten years in which Jews would be the perpetual minority. To achieve the desired population ratio, the White Paper established a limit of Jewish immigration over the next five years to 75,000 persons. While recognizing that Jews were in peril in Europe, the authors of the White Paper placed a higher priority on maintaining peace with the Arabs and, by extension, maintaining the security of the British supply lines through the Middle East to the oil fields of the Persian Gulf, and the resources of British India. Thus, while compassionate British citizens like Sir Nicholas Winton were busy trying to save Jewish children from the Nazis, the British

---

24   "British White Papers: The White Paper of 1939," *Jewish Virtual Library*, https://www.jewishvirtuallibrary.org/british-white-paper-of-1939.

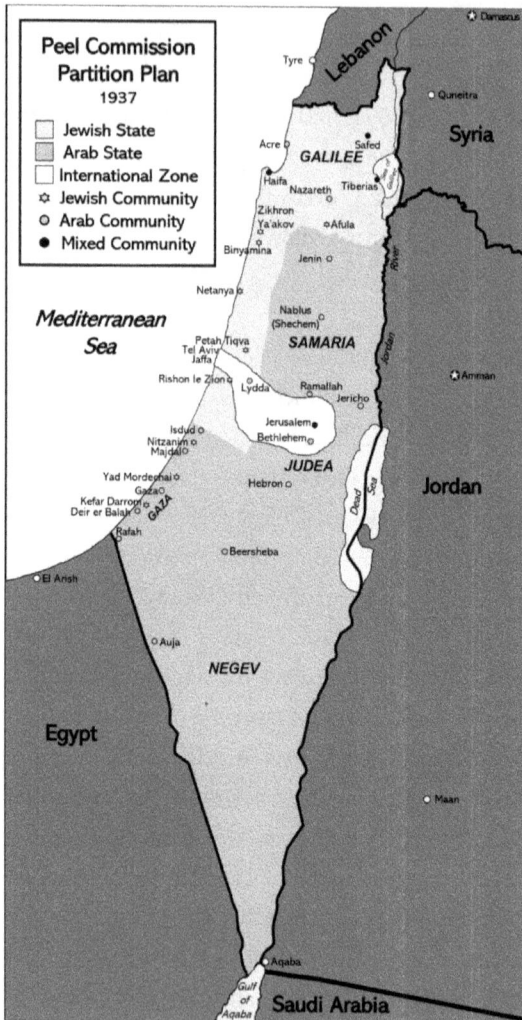

Map 7. Peel Commission Proposal for Partition of Palestine, 1937. (Based on Peel Map, UK Government, Public
domain, via Wikimedia Commons, https://commons.wikimedia.org/wiki/File:PeelMap.png; Peel Map, Ynhockey, Public
domain, via Wikimedia Commons, https://commons.wikimedia.org/wiki/File:Peel_map_pd.png; Map of the 1947
Partition Plan for Palestine by אורי פרקש [Ari Freikas], CC BY-SA 4.0 https://creativecommons.org/licenses/by-sa/4.0, via
Wikimedia Commons, https://commons.wikimedia.org/wiki/File:1947_Partition_plan_for_Palestine_EN.svg

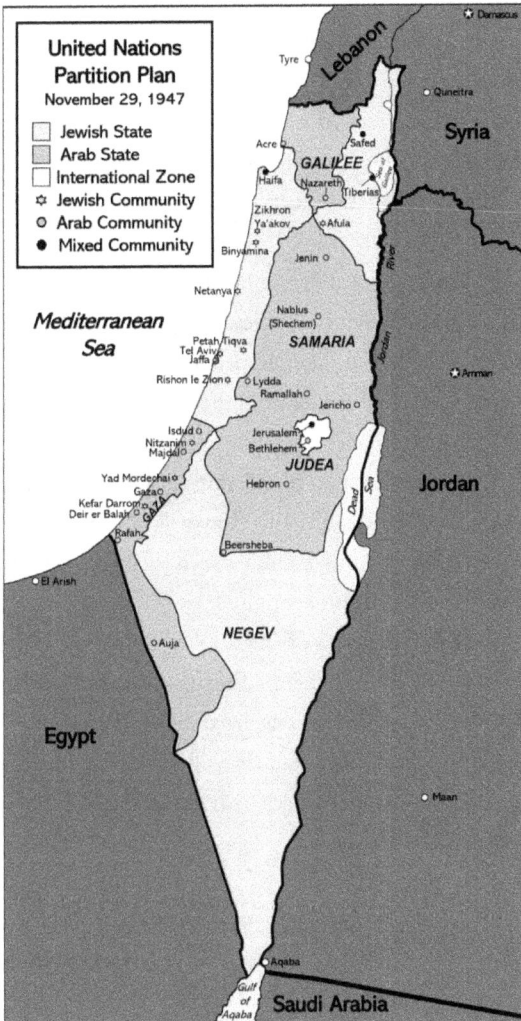

Map 8. United Nations Partition Plan for Palestine, November 29, 1948. (Based on graphic by אורי פרקש (Ari Freikas), אורי פרקש CC BY-SA 4.0 https://creativecommons.org/licenses/by-sa/4.0, via Wikimedia Commons, https://commons.wikimedia.org/wiki/File:1947_Partition_plan_for_Palestine_EN.svg

government was establishing a policy that doomed most of the Jewish population of Europe.[25]

Jewish leaders understood the dire consequences of the White Paper. The response of the Jewish Agency for Palestine outlined those consequences and concluded with a resolute commitment:

> It is in the darkest hour of Jewish history that the British Government proposes to deprive the Jews of their last hope and to close the road back to their Homeland. It is a cruel blow, doubly cruel because it comes from the government of a great nation which has extended a helping hand to the Jews, and whose position must rest on foundations of moral authority and international good faith. This blow will not subdue the Jewish people. The historic bond between the people and the land of Israel cannot be broken. The Jews will never accept the closing to them of the gates of Palestine nor let their national home be converted into a ghetto. The Jewish pioneers who, during the past three generations, have shown their strength in the upbuilding of a derelict country, will from now on display the same strength in defending Jewish immigration, the Jewish home and Jewish freedom.[26]

---

25   In 1939, Nicholas Winton organized the transport of 669 Jewish children from German-occupied Czechoslovakia to Great Britain, where they were taken in by families who cared for them throughout World War II. The outbreak of war in September 1939 brought a halt to the operation. To learn more, see "How Foster Care Saved a Civilization," Albert J. McCarn, *The Barking Fox*, June 30, 2020, https://thebarkingfox.com/2020/06/30/how-foster-care-saved-a-civilization-nations-9th-of-av/.

26   British White Papers: Zionist Reaction to the White Paper, *Jewish Virtual Library*, accessed March 26, 2024, https://www.jewishvirtuallibrary.org/zionist-reaction-to-the-white-paper-of-1939.

This was the situation on the eve of World War II. What followed is well known and beyond dispute: Nazi Germany perpetrated the systematic murder of six million Jews in Europe—a third of the global prewar Jewish population—in what the world knows as the Holocaust and what Jews know as the Shoah (Catastrophe). At the end of that conflict, the survivors had no homes to return to and little hope of making Aliyah to Eretz Israel. At the end of the war, the exhausted British faced a no-win situation, with an increasingly desperate Jewish refugee population seeking refuge in Palestine and an increasingly militant Arab opposition to any further Jewish immigration. As the conflict escalated, the British gave notice to the United Nations that they would surrender the mandate for Palestine in May 1948. That led to the UN General Assembly resolution on November 29, 1947, to partition Palestine into an Arab and a Jewish state (see Map 8, United Nations Partition Plan for Palestine, November 29, 1948). The Jews quickly accepted the plan, but the Arabs rejected it, leaving both sides little alternative but to prepare for war.

The war commenced even before David Ben Gurion declared the independence of the Jewish State of Israel on May 14, 1948. The 650,000 Jewish citizens of the new state faced annihilation as armies from Egypt, Jordan, Syria, Lebanon, and Iraq immediately invaded. God, however, had other plans. Against all odds, Israel defeated every enemy, retained control over West Jerusalem, and proved to the world that the God of Abraham, Isaac, and Jacob still comes through on his promises.[27]

---

27 "Israeli War of Independence: Background & Overview (1947 - 1949)," *Jewish Virtual Library*, https://www.jewishvirtuallibrary.org/background-and-overview-israel-war-of-independence.

Israel still faces overwhelming odds against its survival, surrounded by hostile neighbors on every side and within. The Jewish state could have been wiped off the map more than once, but God intervened, especially in the miraculous victory of 1967 in which Jerusalem, Judea, Samaria, the Golan, Gaza, and the Sinai were liberated from Arab occupation. A further miraculous victory took place in 1973, as the combined forces of Egypt and Syria surprised Israel on Yom Kippur (the Day of Atonement), the holiest day on the Hebrew calendar.

To this day, Arab terrorism, international opposition, blood libels, and anti-Jewish incitement continue to threaten not only the independence of Israel, but also the safety of Jewish communities worldwide. The problem is compounded by continued division among the Jewish body politic, as many still seek assimilation and appeasement even after the horrific massacres inflicted by Hamas and its allies on October 7, 2023.

Can Israel survive? The record of history says it will. God has not failed to preserve a remnant. Over the last 150 years, he has come through with his promises to reestablish Israel and the Jewish people on their ancestral homeland. Every enemy who has opposed them has eventually come to nothing. This is clear from the story of Esther and Mordechai, when God saved the Jewish people from the genocidal plot of Haman. As the tide began to turn against him, Haman's wife and advisors declared, "If Mordecai, before whom you have begun to fall, is of the Jewish people, you will not overcome him but will surely fall before him." (Esther 6:13).

We would do well to remember this counsel. Israel and the Jewish people will face unending threats until Messiah reigns from Zion. We cannot prevent all those troubles, but we can choose which side to take. The course of wisdom is the one Mordechai outlined to Esther:

Do not think to yourself that in the king's palace you will escape any more than all the other Jews. For if you keep silent at this time, relief and deliverance will rise for the Jews from another place, but you and your father's house will perish. And who knows whether you have not come to the kingdom for such a time as this?

—Esther 4:13-14

The choice is whether to bless Abraham's seed or, by inaction, curse them. They will survive regardless, but our outcome may very well depend on what we choose to say and do regarding the Covenant Nation of Israel.

CHAPTER 6

BECAUSE WESTERN CIVILIZATION IS BUILT ON JUDEO-CHRISTIAN VALUES

In January 1918, President Woodrow Wilson delivered a major foreign policy speech in which he introduced his Fourteen Points as the basis for peace negotiations to end World War I. His proposals called for open covenants of peace among nations, freedom of the seas, free trade, international disarmament, national self-determination for ethnic nationalities, and an international body to oversee the affairs of nations. Although the Allies eventually incorporated many of Wilson's points in the peace agreements, they were skeptical at first. One of the most memorable reactions came from French Prime Minister Georges Clemenceau, who remarked, "Quatorze? Le bon Dieu n'a que dix." (Fourteen? The good Lord had only ten.)[1]

Among the revelations we derive from Clemenceau's comment are these: that great leaders of the early 20th century often used snarky comments to make a point, and that they also used biblical references. Those who know their Bibles recognize Clemenceau's reference: he scoffed at Wilson's plan by comparing it to God's instructions for human behavior expressed in the Ten Commandments.

---

1   "President Woodrow Wilson's 14 Points (1918)," *National Archives*, https://www.archives.gov/milestone-documents/president-woodrow-wilsons-14-points, "Woodrow Wilson's 14 Points: A Vision for Post-World War I Peace," *History Tools*, May 26, 2024, https://www.historytools.org/stories/woodrow-wilsons-14-points-a-vision-for-post-world-war-i-peace, Georges Clemenceau, Wikiquote, https://en.wikiquote.org/wiki/Georges_Clemenceau.

What makes Clemenceau's snarky comment even more compelling is its irony: Clemenceau was an atheist. Woodrow Wilson, on the other hand, was a devout Presbyterian who studied the Bible and served as an elder in his church.[2] Given that difference of opinion on spiritual matters, we might wonder how Clemenceau and Wilson, two of the most powerful men in the world at the time, could ever agree on anything—even though the world very much depended on their coming to agreement about how to rebuild the global order after the devastation of the First World War.

Clemenceau and Wilson, along with their counterparts David Lloyd George of Great Britain and Vitorio Orlando of Italy, wrestled with the hard issues of the postwar world at the Paris Peace Conference in 1919. Disagreements abounded, stemming from the national interests of these four major allied powers, as well as the interests of newly independent nations like Poland and Czechoslovakia, and the aspirations of peoples like the Jews, Arabs, Armenians, and Kurds, who desired states of their own. Germany also had aspirations, if only to minimize the sting of defeat and salvage something on which to build a new nation.

Given this maelstrom of competing interests, conflicting agreements, and strong personalities (Clemenceau, for example, was known as "The Tiger"), it is a wonder that the Treaty of Versailles ever came to be. Flawed as it was, the peace agreement of 1919 was a testimony to the values shared by every participant at the Versailles Conference. Most of them were at least nominally Christians, both Catholic and

---

2   Helen M, "Top 10 Facts about Georges Clémenceau," *Discover Walks Blog*, October 22, 2022, https://www.discoverwalks.com/blog/paris/top-10-facts-about-georges-clemenceau/; Cary T. Grayson, "The Religion of Woodrow Wilson," *Cary T. Grayson Papers*, The Woodrow Wilson Presidential Library & Museum, February 3, 1924, https://presidentwilson.org/items/show/22351.

Protestant. Some, like Dr. Chaim Weizmann, were Jewish, and some, like Sherif Faisal, were Muslim.

What values could this diverse gathering of the world's elite possibly have shared?

We could say they shared a regard for life over death, for right over wrong, and for honor and fidelity over faithlessness. Their arguments, pleas, diplomatic maneuvers, and even strong-arm tactics all happened in the context of this shared understanding of how gentlemen, and people in general, should act toward one another.

One description of these shared values is *Judeo-Christian*. With respect to the Muslim, Hindu, Buddhist, Shinto, and other participants at Versailles, they too were operating under this same value system. It is a common standard of behavior for all people—or at least all rational people—that allows us to interact with one another. There are variations on this standard, but the standard itself remains constant, as C.S. Lewis explains:

> I know that some people will say the idea of a Law of Nature or decent behaviour known to all men is unsound, because different civilizations and different ages have had quite different moralities.

> But this is not true. There have been differences between their moralities, but these have never amounted to anything like a total difference. If anyone will take the trouble to compare the moral teaching of, say, the ancient Egyptians, Babylonians, Hindus, Chinese, Greeks and Romans, what will really strike him will be how very like they are to each other and to our own. . . I need only ask the reader to think what a totally different morality would mean. Think of a country where

people were admired for running away in battle, or where a
man felt proud of double-crossing all the people who had been
kindest to him. You might just as well try to imagine a country
where two and two made five.[3]

Lewis goes on to present a logical case for how this value system
common to all humanity points to a Creator, and then makes the case
that the Creator is the God of the Bible. The shared values of humanity,
therefore, are the values God built into us. As we practice them, and
even as we honor them in the breach, we testify to the existence of
the Creator and his desire that we conduct ourselves according to his
standards. That applies both to Jews and Christians, and even to others,
as Paul says:

> For when Gentiles, who do not have the law, by nature do
> what the law requires, they are a law to themselves, even
> though they do not have the law. They show that the work of
> the law is written on their hearts, while their conscience also
> bears witness, and their conflicting thoughts accuse or even
> excuse them on that day when, according to my gospel, God
> judges the secrets of men by Christ Jesus.
> —Romans 2:14-16

These common standards of decency did not come into existence
overnight, or even in a generation. The diverse gathering of delegates at
Versailles could produce a peace treaty because these standards served
as the foundation of their civilization. That foundation was the same

---

3   C.S. Lewis, *Mere Christianity*, The Complete C.S. Lewis Signature Classics (New York:
     HarperCollins, 2002), 17.

one on which the Founders of the American Republic based their arguments for declaring independence from Great Britain:

> When in the Course of human events, it becomes necessary for one people to dissolve the political bands which have connected them with another, and to assume among the powers of the earth, the separate and equal station to which **the Laws of Nature and of Nature's God** entitle them, a decent respect to the opinions of mankind requires that they should declare the causes which impel them to the separation.

> We hold these truths to be self-evident, that **all men are created equal**, that **they are endowed by their Creator with certain unalienable Rights**, that among these are Life, Liberty and the pursuit of Happiness. --**That to secure these rights, Governments are instituted among Men, deriving their just powers from the consent of the governed**, --That whenever any Form of Government becomes destructive of these ends, it is the Right of the People to alter or to abolish it, and to institute new Government, laying its foundation on such principles and organizing its powers in such form, as to them shall seem most likely to effect their Safety and Happiness.[4]

This foundational document testifies to the whole world that the United States of America is a nation established on the Judeo-Christian belief in a single God from whom come all rights, all standards of conduct, and all powers relegated to governments. The government

---

4   *The Declaration of Independence*, July 4, 1776, National Archives, https://www.archives.gov/founding-docs/declaration-transcript (emphasis added).

itself is not God and is not the source of rights and freedoms, but is merely the custodian of those sacred elements of humanity. These are ideas the Founders derived from their understanding of the scriptures as filtered through the Christian expressions of their day. They knew as well that those biblical ideas originated not from the church, but from the Hebrews. We get an indication of that in a letter of February 1809 from John Adams, second President of the United States, to his colleague and successor, Thomas Jefferson:

> I will insist that the Hebrews have done more to civilize men than any other nation. If I were an atheist, and believed in blind eternal fate, I should still believe that fate had ordained the Jews to be the most essential instrument for civilizing nations. If I were an atheist of the other sect, who believe, or pretend to believe, that all is ordered by chance, I should believe that chance had ordered the Jews to preserve and prop-agate to all mankind the doctrine of a supreme, intelligent, wise, almighty Sovereign of the universe, which I believe to be the great essential principle of all morality, and consequently of all civilization. I can not say that I love the Jews very much, nor the French, nor the English, nor the Romans, nor the Greeks. We must love all nations as well as we can, but it is very hard to love most of them.[5]

Adams' admission that he does not "love the Jews very much" is significant. The truth is, we may not "love" someone or something very

---

5   John Adams to Thomas Jefferson, February 1809, Works of John Adams ix. 609-610, quoted in Herbert Friedenwald, "Adams, John," The Jewish Encyclopedia, 1906, vol. 1, p. 184, https://www.jewishencyclopedia.com/articles/767-adams-john.

much, but we can still recognize their status, abilities, qualities, and intrinsic value. In fact, extending such recognition to those we don't like often speaks more powerfully to the characteristics we acknowledge in them. Moreover, Adams' admission is a microcosm of the Christian attitude toward the Jewish people and the Jewish scriptures since the inception of Christianity: acknowledgment of the Jewish roots of our faith and of the civilizational foundation those roots have produced for us all, while simultaneously maintaining our distance from anything Jewish.

This is another irony: Christians have adopted and profess to live by the standards of conduct articulated by Moses, but we have simultaneously professed to be "free from the Law" because of what Christ did on the cross. In truth, it's really a matter of degree. For all the differences of festive celebrations, calendar observance, and ritual, Christians and Jews still uphold the same moral standards articulated by Moses, lived by Jesus, and preached by the Prophets and Apostles.

Dennis Prager, the Jewish author and columnist, lists ten shared values of Christians and Jews that bring them into alignment on social issues:

1. There is one God. That God is the God introduced to the world by the Hebrew Bible—the source of one universal morality.

2. The Hebrew Bible (the only Bible Jesus knew and which he frequently cited) introduced the most revolutionary moral idea in history: that there are objective moral truths just as there are mathematical and scientific truths. Without God as the source of moral standards, there is no moral truth; there are only moral opinions.

3. Because there are moral truths, good and evil are the same for all people.

4. God—not man, not government, not popular opinion, not a democratic vote—is the source of our rights. All men "are endowed by their Creator with certain unalienable Rights," declares the American Declaration of Independence.

5. The human being is "created in the image of God." There-fore, each human life is precious. Therefore, race is of no significance, since we are all created in God's image and God has no race.

6. The world is based on a divine order, meaning divinely ordained distinctions. Among these divine distinctions are God and man, man and woman, human and animal, good and evil, nature and God, and the holy and the profane.

7. Man is not basically good. Christians speak of "original sin" in referring to man's sinful nature; Jews cite God Himself in Genesis: "The will of man's heart is evil from his youth" (Genesis 8:21). They are not identical beliefs, but they are both worlds apart from the naive Enlightenment belief that man is basically good. And they come to the same conclusion: we need God-based rules to keep us from our natural inclination to do evil.

8. Therefore, we must not follow our hearts. Both religious Jews and Christians are keenly aware of how morally dan-gerous it is to be led by our emotions. Those who reject

Judeo-Christian values are far more likely to follow and promote the advice, "Follow your heart."

9. God gave us the Ten Commandments—the core of Judeo-Christian values. Therefore, to apply but one of the Ten Commandments to our morally confused secular age, you must "Honor your father and mother" even if they voted for someone you loathe—meaning, at the least, remain in contact with them and do not dare deprive them of the right to be in contact with their grandchildren.

10. Human beings have free will. In the secular world, there is no free will because all human behavior is attributed to biology and environment. Only a religious worldview, because it posits the existence of a divine soul—something independent of biology and environment—allows for free will.[6]

Prager goes on to explain how Judaism and Christianity need each other:

> Without the Old Testament, there is no New Testament. **Virtually every Christian moral principle derives from the Hebrew Bible**—not only the 10 Judeo-Christian values enumerated here, but such basic moral principles as "Love your neighbor as yourself (Leviticus 19:18), "Love the Lord your God with all your heart …" (Deuteronomy 6:5), and "Love the stranger" (Deuteronomy 10:19).

---

6   Dennis Prager, "What Are Judeo-Christian Values?" *North State Journal*, February 26, 2023, https://nsjonline.com/article/2023/02/prager-what-are-judeo-christian-values/.

At the same time, Judaism needs Christians. **It was Christianity that carried the Torah and the rest of the Hebrew Bible to the world**. This was acknowledged by the greatest Jewish thinker after Moses, Maimonides.[7]

The biblical foundation of Western Civilization is beyond dispute. Our Judeo-Christian foundation upholds the rule of law, the intrinsic value of human beings, the sanctity of life, the preservation of property, and the existence of national boundaries. In other words, Judeo-Christian values uphold a global order comprised of self-governing nation-states, which in turn are comprised of self-governing, moral individuals.

It is no overstatement that the continued existence of Israel and the Jewish people is essential to the continued existence of our civilization. If, God forbid, Israel's enemies succeeded in eradicating the Jewish state, and if somehow every vestige of Judaism and of the Jewish people were assimilated or otherwise disappeared, God's values as articulated in the Bible and lived out for millennia by Jews and Christians would not immediately disappear. God would somehow work miracles to make sure this foundation remained intact—perhaps even by bringing about the long-expected Messianic Age.

Think, however, what it means to oppose this godly foundation of Judeo-Christian values and the Jewish people who are the custodians of those values (Romans 3:1-2). Claiming that the Jewish people are "cursed of God," or that they are colonial, apartheid occupiers of Arab land, or that they have no right to live in their ancestral homeland is essentially saying that God is wrong and made a mistake by keeping the Jewish people in existence all these centuries. If God were wrong about that, or if somehow he decided that the Jewish people were no

---

7   Ibid., emphasis added.

longer worthy of his promises to restore them completely, then can we trust God on *any* matter? Why should we continue to uphold the standards of righteousness we claim God has articulated if he made those standards optional and then abandoned the Jewish people for opting not to follow them?

This is a slippery slope of logic that might very well lead us to that place Christians have dreaded for centuries:

> Let no one deceive you in any way. For that day will not come, unless the rebellion comes first, and the man of lawlessness is revealed, the son of destruction, who opposes and exalts himself against every so-called god or object of worship, so that he takes his seat in the temple of God, proclaiming himself to be God. Do you not remember that when I was still with you I told you these things? And you know what is restraining him now so that he may be revealed in his time. For the mystery of lawlessness is already at work. Only he who now restrains it will do so until he is out of the way.
> —2 Thessalonians 2:3-8

Could it be that God is working through the Jewish people as his agents of restraint for this "mystery of lawlessness"? Maybe the restraint is the Judeo-Christian values system, which is based on the Law of Moses. Maybe the strength of that system comes from the way its practitioners support one another. If one turns on the other, is that not itself a manifestation of lawlessness? Perhaps this is another level of meaning in Paul's exhortation to Gentile followers of Jesus. If, as he says, we are grafted into the olive tree of Israel, then we should take seriously his declaration that we don't support the root, but the root supports us (Romans 11:16-18).

CHAPTER 7

BECAUSE ISRAEL SHINES THE LIGHT OF FREEDOM IN A VERY DARK NEIGHBORHOOD

Those who have never visited the world's only Jewish state may be surprised at the diversity on display everywhere. A stroll through the streets of Jerusalem or Tel Aviv brings encounters with Jewish citizens of all colors, with origins in Europe, the Americas, North Africa, Iran, Iraq, Yemen, Ethiopia, India, and East Asia. There will also be encounters with Arab and Druze citizens and residents, as well as foreign workers from Thailand, the Philippines, and many other nations. Those are the people who live in Israel. There are also millions of tourists, nonprofit volunteers, corporate executives, technical experts, and students who extend the spectrum of diversity even further, testifying to the fact that Israel is literally a crossroads of the entire world.

The spiritual diversity of Israel is an aspect casual visitors might miss. They may expect to see Judaism in its many forms, especially in Jerusalem. Observant Jews, meaning those who know the Bible and live by it, are as varied as devout Christians. Many wear distinctive clothing, even if it seems more appropriate to the colder climates of Europe than to the year-round hot weather of Israel. Their lifestyles reflect their biblical worldview, which incorporates varying degrees of interpretation about applying Torah principles to daily life. The Ultra-Orthodox (Haredi), for instance, are very strict about separating themselves from secular society, which becomes a political issue at times on questions such as exemption from military conscription for Haredi students at Yeshiva (institutions of Jewish religious study).

Since Israel is the world's only Jewish state, Jewish religious expression is everywhere, especially at the Kotel (Western Wall) in Jerusalem. Everyone is welcome to pray there, even if they are not Jewish. It is a picture of what we can expect in time (perhaps sooner than we think) when the Lord's House is a house of prayer for all nations (Isaiah 56:6-7; Mark 11:17). I have prayed there many times, joining with crowds of Jewish and Christian worshippers who come to this holy place every day of the year. On other occasions, I have joined with observant Jews—Ashkenazi, Sephardi, and Teimani (Yemenite)—in celebrating the feasts of the Lord and observing the fast of the 9th of Av.

That's just the Jewish aspect of Israel's spiritual diversity. Muslims worship freely as well. The prayer calls from the minarets sound throughout the land five times each day, even from the mosques atop the Temple Mount. Bells also ring out from the multitude of Christian churches and institutions all over Israel. Christian worship is vibrant at Christ Church in Jerusalem, and there I have joined with other Christians and Messianic Jews in praising God and our Savior Jesus. Catholic, Orthodox, and Armenian clergy roam Jerusalem's Old City, and their churches are open to all visitors. One of the most interesting encounters I remember was at Mount Carmel, the traditional site where Elijah confronted the prophets of Baal (1 Kings 18). On the day of my first visit there, a group of Korean Christians knelt in fervent intercession, praying both in Korean and in tongues. Their highly charged charismatic prayer was not out of place, although it did invite puzzled glances from visitors affiliated with less demonstrative sects.

This diversity might seem peculiar for a nation accused by some of practicing apartheid against its Arab citizens and residents.[1] They co

---

1   "Israel's Apartheid Against Palestinians: A Look into Decades of Oppression and

prise 21.4% of Israel's population of nearly 10 million. Jews, of course, comprise 78.6% of the population, of whom over 500,000 live in what some consider to be "occupied Palestinian territories" of the West Bank and East Jerusalem.[2] As we now know, those territories are actually the ancestral Jewish biblical heartland of Judea and Samaria. Still, Arab families live there, and many have lived there for generations—as have Arab families in the rest of Israel. Are those families and their communities truly afflicted by a Jewish colonialist oppressor?

If they are, then why are Arab political parties permitted to run candidates for office? Why do those Arab parties have elected members of the Knesset (Israel's parliament)? In fact, if Israel truly were an apartheid state, why would some of those Arab parties be allowed to join a governing coalition, as the United Arab List (Ra'am) did in 2022?[3] Why also would Israel permit Arabs—both Christian and Muslim—to serve as judges at all levels, including Israel's Supreme Court?[4]

We might also ask why the military and police forces of Israel actively recruit minorities into the ranks. These are not conscripts, but volunteers. Jewish men and women are subject to the military draft, but the ranks are open to all others. The Israel Defense Forces (IDF) integrates Jews, Druze, Muslims, Arabs, Bedouins, and Christians, making

Domination," *Amnesty International*, February 1, 2022, https://www.amnesty.org/en/latest/campaigns/2022/02/israels-system-of-apartheid/.

2   "Vital Statistics: Latest Population Statistics for Israel (October 1, 2024)," *Jewish Virtual Library*, https://www.jewishvirtuallibrary.org/latest-population-statistics-for-israel#ultra.

3   Gil Hoffman, "Lapid tells Rivlin: I have succeeded in forming coalition with Bennett," *The Jerusalem Post*, Jun 3, 2021, https://www.jpost.com/israel-news/politics-and-diplomacy/lapid-tells-rivlin-new-government-ready-669937.

4   "Khaled Kabub sworn in as Israeli Supreme Court's first Muslim justice," *The Times of Israel*, May 9, 2022, https://www.timesofisrael.com/khaled-kabub-sworn-in-as-supreme-courts-first-muslim-justice/.

it an army that represents the entire population. This is intentional; Israel seeks to build a force that all Israelis, of all ethnicities and sects, can trust and be proud of. That effort is succeeding, as evident in the increased recruitment levels among minorities, particularly the Druze, of whom about 80% of young men volunteer for military service. Ella Waweya, the first Arab Muslim woman to attain the rank of major in the IDF, explains why they serve:

> What are people looking for? Equality between an Arab and a
> Jew, a Bedouin, a Druze and a Christian. The path to equality
> passes through the IDF, the Ministry of Defense, and the
> police. That's how it starts.[5]

Major Waweywa's comment, coming from her personal experience, speaks to the nation-building function of institutions like the army. Such institutions bring together diverse segments of the population, creating a space where they can find ways to bridge their differences and discover the unity they share as members of the same nation. That not only establishes unity among the different ethnic and religious segments of Israeli society, but within each segment as well. For example, Israel's Jewish warriors come from every segment of Jewish society: secular, Orthodox, Haredi, Karaite, and Messianic. Outside the army, the divisions among these segments cause fault lines that occasionally rock the fabric of the state, but all find reason to uphold the army. It's not merely that their sons and daughters serve in the ranks, both on

---

5   Quoted in Suzan Quitaz, "Exclusive: IDF - 'Our Mission is to Enlist as Many Israeli
     Arabs as we can,'" *Al Majalla*, July 8, 2022, https://en.majalla.com/node/237956/
     politicsexclusive-idf-%E2%80%93-%E2%80%98our-mission-enlist-many-israeli-arabs-
     we-can%E2%80%99.

active duty and as reserve soldiers, but that the IDF is an institution that has consistently served all Israel with honor from the earliest days of independence.

Again, this is more than a Jewish Israeli phenomenon. Major Waweya provides an inclusive perspective that addresses what the army means to all Israelis:

> I am a woman, an Arab, a Muslim, an Israeli, and an officer in the IDF. This truly shows the democracy of our country, of our culture here, that we can all be here together. The truth is never only one-sided. I say to everyone out there: "Come and visit Israel, no matter your language or religion. Come to our beautiful country for a few days and understand what is going on in Lebanon; understand why our war is just." Let them go and walk around in Judea and Samaria and see what happens if you say that you're Jewish, and they'll understand straight away how much we must fight to keep the Jewish people in the State of Israel safe. I say this as a Muslim: We know how to live together, and that's how it should be. We need to help each other and remain together. It's especially fun to walk around Israel and hear all the languages and see the diversity. Israel is not only about a conflict between Arabs and Jews. Israel is fun. And even when there are frictions it's because we are one family, as we saw in this war which reunited us. This is the title of the State of Israel—a family. So, it's no wonder that people call each other "brother" in the streets.[6]

---

6   Major Ella Waweywa quoted in Ohad Merlin, "Meet Ella Waweya, the IDF's top Muslim woman, speaking out to the Arab world - exclusive," *The Jerusalem Post*, July 13, 2024, https://www.jpost.com/israel-hamas-war/article-809892.

Israel is not unique in accepting the service of women in the military. What is unique is that Israel actively recruits not only women, but people of every religious and ethnic minority. That's not normal in a repressive regime that seeks to dominate its population. Tyrants routinely employ strong-arm tactics to keep troublesome populations under control. That is why the governments of Turkey, Syria, Iraq, and Iran routinely mount military operations against their minority Kurdish populations. Those same governments repress Christian minorities, to the point that Iraq's Christian population has decreased 80% from 1.4 million in 1987 to about 250,000 in 2019.[7] The same could be said of any minority group, such as the Druze of Syria, the Armenians of Turkey, the Copts of Egypt, the Christian Africans of Sudan, and others. The Arab regimes even persecute one another, particularly if it is a matter of Shi'a and Sunni Muslims continuing the centuries-old feud between the two major divisions of Islam.

Who would know this better than Benjamin Netanyahu? Having served Israel since the 1970s as a soldier, diplomat, Knesset member, and three terms as prime minister, he understands the difference between Israel's democratic institutions and the repressive regimes of Israel's neighbors. In 1999, six years before Israel's unilateral withdrawal from Gaza, Netanyahu wrote:

> It is little consolation that most of the movements for
> "democracy" in the Arab world, such as in Algeria and Jordan,
> are dominated by Moslem [sic] fundamentalists seeking

---

7   Stephen Kahn, "Pope's upcoming visit brings attention to the dwindling population of Christians in Iraq," *The Conversation*, March 3, 2021, https://theconversation.com/popes-upcoming-visit-brings-attention-to-the-dwindling-population-of-christians-in-iraq-152421.

not to break down and distribute the government's absolute
monopoly of power but to transfer that power—to themselves.
With opponents such as these, it is difficult to judge which is
more oppressive, the people's current rulers or their would-be
liberators. The difficulty is greatest in Lebanon, where a
kaleidoscope of armed gangs of various persuasions have for
two decades competed for the right to brutalize the country.
This nightmare out of Hobbes has finally been ended only
through the imposition of an even more ruthless Pax Syri-
ana—a "peace" extorted through the application of limitless
fear. Remove the Syrian boot, and the internecine violence will
be unleashed again.[8]

Netanyahu goes on to document the violence Arab regimes have
perpetrated against one another and against their own populations for
generations. The Palestinian factions are no different. From the beginning of Arab resistance to the establishment of the Jewish homeland
under the British Mandate in Palestine, the greatest threat to the Palestinian Arab population has not been the Jewish population and its government institutions, but rather strong men like Haj Amin al-Husayni,
Yasser Arafat, and Yahya Sinwar who built their power base on opposition to the Jewish state. Their first targets were not Jews, but their
own Arab neighbors—Muslim and Christian—who opposed them. As
Netanyahu states, this was a pattern established from the beginning:

[Haj Amin al-Husayni] was appointed Grand Mufti of
Jerusalem by the British in 1921, less than a year after they

---

8   Benjamin Netanyahu, *A Durable Peace: Israel and Its Place Among the Nations* (New York: Warner Books, 2000), 106.

convicted him for instigating the murderous anti-Jewish riots in the Old City of Jerusalem. The Mufti's incitement and organization of enforcement gangs to back his ideas led to even more severe anti-Jewish riots across Palestine in 1921, then to the greatest massacres of August 1929. But the Mufti's main targets were actually Arabs. With his henchman Emil Ghouri and with funding from the Nazis and Italian Fascists, he organized the torture and murder of moderate Arab leaders, landowners willing to sell to Jews, and anyone else he believed had betrayed his virulent creed.[9]

Things have not changed in the intervening century. Moderate voices among the Palestinian Arabs, and in the surrounding nations, have faced greater censure from their own, often self-appointed, leaders than from the Israelis. It is true that Israel places great restrictions on Arabs living in Judea, Samaria, and Gaza, but with good reason. The checkpoints, military incursions, surveillance, and other measures exist because Arab leaders since the 1920s have sought to annihilate the Jewish presence in the land of Israel rather than find ways to live in peace.

They could easily have found peace and achieved prosperity for their people, just as the multitudes of Arab Israelis have done for generations. The Jewish people have continuously held out their hands in offers of peace, both as a nation and as individuals, from the beginning. That is why the Jewish State has readily agreed to arrangements for sharing the land, from the division of the original Palestinian Mandate in 1922 down to the Trump "Deal of the Century" peace plan in 2020. It's why activist Israelis like Vivian Silver dedicated their lives to

---

9   Ibid., 206.

building peaceful relationships with their Arab neighbors. As one of the founding members of Women Wage Peace, Silver would drive sick Gazans to Israeli hospitals for treatment. Tragically, Silver was among the casualties when the terrorist flood from Gaza overran her community of Be'eri on October 7, 2023.[10]

Israel is certainly not a perfect place to live, and it is not the righteous nation God has intended it to be since he called Abraham to father it. That is why devout Christians and Jews alike question and criticize Israel's liberal policy on abortion, and openness to alternative lifestyles that have made Tel Aviv one of the most "gay friendly" cities in the world.[11] The righteous shake their heads and pray for revival, but even this speaks to Israel's light shining in a dark neighborhood. LGBTQ+ people are not welcome in strict Muslim societies. Conservative Jews and Christians do not agree with their life choices, but they are not about to have them hanged or thrown off a roof as happens in fundamentalist Muslim societies.[12]

This is what Israel stands against. In the beginning, the Zionist dream sought the return of Jews to their ancestral homeland so that they could be free and live in peace. That dream has expanded to embrace all Israelis: Jew and Arab, Druze and Bedouin, secular and religious, liberal and conservative. It's more than simply the only democracy in

---

10   Rami Amichay, "'The peace movement was orphaned', says son of activist killed on Oct. 7," *Reuters*, November 16, 2023, https://www.reuters.com/world/the-peace-movement-was-orphaned-says-son-activist-killed-oct-7-2023-11-16/.

11   "Is Tel Aviv the gay capital of the world?" *The Jerusalem Post*, February 14, 2023, https://www.jpost.com/israel-news/culture/article-731595.

12   Graeme Reid, "Islamic State's War on Gays," *Human Rights Watch*, June 8, 2015, https://www.hrw.org/news/2015/06/08/islamic-states-war-gays; Joe McCarthy, "These 6 Countries Execute People for Being Gay," https://www.globalcitizen.org/en/content/these-6-countries-execute-people-for-being-gay/

the Middle East. Israel is a light of freedom, life, and peace in a dark neighborhood that has known little more than tyrannical despots since time immemorial.

CHAPTER 8

BECAUSE CHRISTIAN SUPPORT FOR ISRAEL IS PROPHESIED

What I learned about prophecy in my Christian upbringing emphasized that God would make it happen in time. The focus of eschatology, as I received it, was on the return of Jesus. Prophetic analysis and
interpretation delved into the "signs of the times" described in passages
like Matthew 24 and 2 Timothy 3:1-9, continually seeking correlations
to current events to gauge how far the prophetic clock had advanced
toward the unknown day and hour when the Messiah would return to
set everything right.

That made sense until I met my first Jewish Israeli friend. She was
instrumental in helping me understand the blind spots in my Evangelical eschatology. It all began when we were attending a conference on
Christian-Jewish relations, where she was the only Orthodox Jewish
participant. At one point, she remarked that, from a Jewish perspective, Christians seemed to want all the Jews to return to Israel solely to
trigger the Rapture. Then, the Christians would go to heaven while the
Jews were stuck on earth to go through the Tribulation, during which
two-thirds of them would die.

My friend's assessment struck me like a lightning bolt. I realized
she was right and that my years of fascination with prophecy—always
with the Jewish people at the center—revolved around the expectations
she had just articulated. That's when I realized that there must be more
to biblical prophecies of the End Times than what I had learned.

Since then, other Jewish friends have helped me understand a key
difference in the Jewish approach to prophecy: while we Christians

see it as an unalterable series of events God will bring about, Jews see prophecy as a job description.

An amusing anecdote illustrates this difference. It concerns a pastor and a rabbi who led a discussion on messianic prophecy with a mixed Christian and Jewish audience. At one point, they were asked about Zechariah's famous prophecy indicating where Messiah would arrive:

> On that day his feet shall stand on the Mount of Olives that
> lies before Jerusalem on the east, and the Mount of Olives shall
> be split in two from east to west by a very wide valley, so that
> one half of the Mount shall move northward, and the other
> half southward.
> —Zechariah 14:4

The pastor said, "This tells us where Messiah will come, but doesn't tell us when. We should pray for revelation about that."

The rabbi said, "Now that we know where Messiah will arrive and what will happen when he's here, maybe we should all get shovels and start digging to prepare the ground."

This Jewish approach to prophecy is distilled in the statement, "If not us, who? If not now, when?" The original quote is attributed to the sage Hillel the Elder,[1] and is recorded in *Pirkei Avot* (The Ethics of the Fathers):

---

1   Rabbi Neal J. Loevinger, "If Not Now, When? Rashi understands Moses' final words to the people as an expression of Hillel's philosophy of self-examination," *My Jewish Learning*, https://www.myjewishlearning.com/article/if-not-now-when/. The quote from *Pirkei Avot* is from the Mishnah Yomit translation by Dr. Joshua Kulp, available on Sefaria.org at https://www.sefaria.org/Pirkei_Avot.1?lang=bi.

If I am not for myself, who is for me? But if I am for my own
self [only], what am I? And if not now, when?
—Pirkei Avot 1:14

Hillel's adage has come down to us through Jewish, Christian, and
now popular culture as a call to action. When it comes to biblical sub-
jects such as prophecy, it is a challenge to evaluate how this prophecy
applies to us now in our day. That is the same thing Isaiah did when he
encountered the Lord:

And I heard the voice of the Lord saying, "Whom shall I send,
and who will go for us?" Then I said, "Here I am! Send me."
—Isaiah 6:8

When it comes to prophecies about Israel's restoration, what could
possibly apply to Christians? Much, actually. Just about everything
God has said about Israel's regathering, restoration, and final redemption has direct application to Christians as well as to Jews.

It may be a surprise to learn that the topic most frequently addressed
in prophecy from Genesis to Revelation is not Messiah's coming and
return, but rather Israel's restoration. Messiah's role is rightly understood in this context. We know that Jesus is the Jewish Messiah of Israel
and of the nations. His priority was on the regathering of the lost sheep
of the house of Israel (Matthew 10:5-6, 15:24). That was the context
in which Jesus gave instructions to his disciples when he first sent them
to minister in his name:

These twelve Jesus sent out, instructing them, "Go nowhere
among the Gentiles and enter no town of the Samaritans, but
go rather to the lost sheep of the house of Israel. And proclaim

> as you go, saying, 'The kingdom of heaven is at hand.' Heal
> the sick, raise the dead, cleanse lepers, cast out demons. You
> received without paying; give without pay. Acquire no gold or
> silver or copper for your belts, no bag for your journey, or two
> tunics or sandals or a staff, for the laborer deserves his food."
> —Matthew 10:5-10

These instructions are still valid for us today. While the church has done well in spreading the gospel of salvation in Jesus to the ends of the earth, it has often overlooked that the ultimate goal of this gospel is not merely individual salvation but the establishment of the kingdom of heaven—the very kingdom referred to in scripture as Zion and Israel. The Messiah is king of Israel, as proclaimed on the day he entered Jerusalem, his capital city, in triumph:

> Now when they drew near to Jerusalem and came to Beth-
> phage, to the Mount of Olives, then Jesus sent two disciples,
> saying to them, "Go into the village in front of you, and
> immediately you will find a donkey tied, and a colt with her.
> Untie them and bring them to me. If anyone says anything
> to you, you shall say, 'The Lord needs them,' and he will send
> them at once." This took place to fulfill what was spoken by
> the prophet, saying, "Say to the daughter of Zion, 'Behold,
> your king is coming to you, humble, and mounted on a
> donkey, on a colt, the foal of a beast of burden.'"
> —Matthew 21:1-5 (cf. Zechariah 9:9 and Isaiah 63:11)

The fact that many of the Jewish people of that generation did not receive Jesus as Messiah does not change or diminish these eternal promises of God. In fact, as Paul explains, that very development is what opened the way for people from the nations (Gentiles) to come into the kingdom:

> So I ask, did they stumble in order that they might fall? By no means! Rather, through their trespass salvation has come to the Gentiles, so as to make Israel jealous. Now if their trespass means riches for the world, and if their failure means riches for the Gentiles, how much more will their full inclusion mean!
> —Romans 11:11-12

What I have usually heard about this passage is that Christians are supposed to "make Israel jealous" by telling Jewish people about their Messiah so that they can learn what they missed and finally accept Jesus as their savior. This interpretation has reduced the gospel of the kingdom to individual salvation, which is a valid aspect of the gospel. However, this "reductionist gospel" largely falls on deaf ears when presented to Jewish people. Jews who know their Bible are expecting Messiah's coming to coincide with the final redemption of Israel as a nation. That is a subject of which many Christians are ignorant. Once we understand the wider context of the Messianic prophecies, then we realize how "making Israel jealous" means those of us from the nations who have attached ourselves to the God of Israel are supposed to lead the way in the restoration of Israel.

There is, of course, a spiritual aspect to this restoration process. Zechariah has something to say about that:

> "Thus says the LORD of hosts: Peoples shall yet come, even the inhabitants of many cities. The inhabitants of one city shall go to another, saying, 'Let us go at once to entreat the favor of the LORD and to seek the LORD of hosts; I myself am

going.' Many peoples and strong nations shall come to seek
the LORD of hosts in Jerusalem and to entreat the favor of the
LORD. Thus says the LORD of hosts: In those days ten men
from the nations of every tongue shall take hold of the robe of
a Jew, saying, 'Let us go with you, for we have heard that God
is with you.'"
—Zechariah 8:20-23

Notice the specificity of this prophecy regarding people from the
nations approaching Jewish people and encouraging them to go with
them to Jerusalem to seek the Lord. That tells us, first of all, that God
still regards the physical city of Jerusalem in the physical land of Israel
as his special place to meet with us all. Second, it tells us that God
intends to keep working in and through the Jewish people to bring
about the spiritual awakening of people from all nations.

A Christian understanding of this passage is that those of us from
the nations have already taken hold of the garment of a particular Jew,
meaning Jesus Christ, and that through him we have access to the holy
place where God dwells. That is definitely true from a spiritual perspective. Let's consider it now from a physical perspective.

Christians care for the Jewish people because our Jewish Messiah
cares for them. Because of what we learned from Jesus and his Jewish
apostles, we know that the Jewish people, as the visible remnant of Israel,
are to experience a great spiritual awakening in the process of Israel's
restoration. Even before this awakening, God was at work regathering
and restoring them to the Promised Land, resurrecting their independent nation, and stirring their hearts to walk out the promises of God
as his chosen people. God invites us to take part in this miraculous
process by recognizing his presence among his people and encouraging
them to be the Jewish lions he has called them to be. It is we who are

supposed to exhort them to greater spiritual heights by obeying God's commandments. Along the way, our testimony in Messiah plays a role, not in requiring our Jewish brethren to convert to Christianity and walk away from Torah, but to be true to their calling and follow the Torah to the full revelation of Messiah (Galatians 3:23-29).

Zechariah's prophecy looks forward to the time when the Temple is rebuilt in Jerusalem and functioning as a house of prayer for all nations (Isaiah 56:6-7, Matthew 21:12-13, Mark 11:17). Much has to happen before that occurs, but much has already happened. The nations are already involved in the process and have been instrumental in carrying out their assigned roles in promises from Isaiah like these:

> Thus says the Lord GOD: "Behold, I will lift up my hand to the nations, and raise my signal to the peoples; and they shall bring your sons in their arms, and your daughters shall be carried on their shoulders. Kings shall be your foster fathers, and their queens your nursing mothers. With their faces to the ground they shall bow down to you, And lick the dust of your feet. Then you will know that I am the LORD; those who wait for me shall not be put to shame."
> —Isaiah 49:22-23

Gentiles, and specifically Christians, have been involved in these very actions from the earliest days of the Zionist movement. Christians have inspired and encouraged the Zionist vision, advocated for Israel, assisted Jews making Aliyah, supported Jewish farmers, and more. Benjamin Netanyahu documents this instrumental Christian role in the Zionist cause, noting how it coincided with the secular humanist Jewish origins of modern Zionism:

With this humanist stream converged another important current that became ascendant in the [19th] century—that of Christian Zionism, a movement that promoted the belief that the spiritual redemption of mankind could occur only if it were preceded by the ingathering of the Jewish exiles, as foretold in the Bible. After all, to both Christians and Jews, Zionism was the fulfillment of ancient prophecy. "[He] will assemble the outcasts of Israel and gather together the dispersed of Judea from the four corners of the earth," said Isaiah. "He that scattered Israel will gather him," promised Jeremiah. "For I will take you from among the nations and gather you out of all countries and will bring you into your own land," Ezekiel foretold.[2]

He goes on to say:

The writings, philanthropic activities, exhortations, and explorations of non-Jewish Zionists, British and American, secular and religious, directly influenced the thinking of such pivotal statesmen as [British Prime Minister] David Lloyd George, [British Foreign Minister] Arthur Balfour, and [US President] Woodrow Wilson at the beginning of the [20th] century. These were all broadly educated men, and they were intimately familiar with the decline of Palestine and the agonized history of the Jews. "My anxiety," wrote Balfour, "is simply to find some means by which the present dreadful state of so large a proportion of the Jewish race . . . may be brought to an end."

---

2   Netanyahu, *A Durable Peace*, 17-18. Netanyahu's biblical references are Isaiah 11:12, Jeremiah 31:10, and Ezekiel 36:24.

Thus, it was the non-Jewish Zionism of Western statesmen that aided Jewish Zionism in achieving the rebirth of Israel.[3]

In a very real sense, as Netanyahu documents, kings served as the foster fathers of modern Israel and their queens as Israel's nursing mothers. That trend continued through President Harry Truman, who led the world in recognizing the new State of Israel in 1948, and President Donald Trump, who recognized Jerusalem as Israel's undivided capital in 2017.

That is the work of the great and powerful, we might say, but people like Truman and Lloyd George would not have described themselves in that way. They simply followed the directions of their God, answering his call to action in the same way Isaiah did—"Here I am! Send me!" The same could be said of Dean Bye, a Canadian businessman who, with his wife, Patti, founded Return Ministries, an organization dedicated to helping Jews make Aliyah to Israel and, through the Aliyah Return Center, get established in their new home.[4] It could also be said of Tommy and Sherri Waller, farmers from Tennessee who founded HaYovel, an organization that brings Christian volunteers from all over the world to help Jewish farmers in Judea and Samaria. The story of HaYovel's founding speaks directly to the prophesied role of Christians from the nations in Israel's restoration:

---

3   Ibid, 22.

4   Return Ministries, https://www.return.co.il/; Aliyah Return Center, https://aliyahreturncenter.com/. To hear Dean Bye tell the story of how and why he became involved in helping Jews return to Israel and become established there, listen to Dean Bye, "Partners in Redemption," interview by Albert J. McCarn, *Reunion Roadmap Israel Connections*, June 11, 2023, audio, https://www.buzzsprout.com/2292194/episodes/14329852.

In 2004, a Christian farmer from Tennessee met Nir Lavi, an Israeli, Orthodox Jewish, vineyard owner. Little did they know, this meeting would begin a movement that would forever change Christian involvement in the prophetic restoration of the land of Israel. Nir's vineyards are located in Samaria, the biblical heartland of Israel, a place many incorrectly refer to as the West Bank.

Nir took Tommy to the edge of his fledgling vineyard and opened his Bible to Jeremiah 31:5: "*You shall again plant vineyards on the mountains of Samaria, the planters shall plant and eat them as ordinary food.*"

Tommy was overwhelmed. He was standing in a vineyard on the mountains of Samaria, planted by a Jewish man, exactly as the Prophet Jeremiah prophesied three thousand years before! He realized that he was looking at modern-day prophecy in action. In a moment of awe, he turned to Nir and asked, "What can we do to help?"[5]

That was the inspiration that moved the Wallers to begin a work that has literally fulfilled another biblical prophecy:

Strangers shall stand and tend your flocks; foreigners shall be your plowmen and vinedressers.
—Isaiah 61:5

---

5 "The Story of HaYovel's Founding," *HaYovel*, https://serveisrael.com/vision-and-mission/.

The story of Christian Zionists is even more vibrant today than it was in the decades leading up to Israel's rebirth. Their predecessors in this work include not only the great statesmen but also the Righteous Among the Nations who risked everything to save Jews out of the Holocaust. Their stories are recorded at Yad Vashem, the World Holocaust Remembrance Center.[6] Some of these heroes are well known, such as Corrie Ten Boom. She and her family hid Jews in their home in the Netherlands, but eventually, the Ten Booms were betrayed to the Nazis and arrested. Corrie survived the ordeal, but her father and sister did not. Another hero was Raoul Wallenberg, a Swedish diplomat who rescued many Hungarian Jews before he was taken into custody and disappeared. Then there was Master Sergeant Roddie Edmonds, an American prisoner of war who took decisive action to save the Jewish soldiers under his command in a German prison camp. Another example of Righteous Gentiles is the entire resistance movement of Denmark, who saved almost all their Jewish fellow citizens in the autumn of 1943 by smuggling them into neutral Sweden.[7]

One lesson we learn from these who walked out their prophetic destiny is that they did so regardless whether their governments or the nations of the earth helped or hindered them. The greatest stories of faith come from those who opposed the policies of their governments, the hostility of the nations toward Israel, and even the conventional wisdom of friends and neighbors. Collectively, their efforts over the years have not only saved Jewish people from death, but also

6   "The Righteous Among the Nations," https://www.yadvashem.org/righteous.html.

7   Cornelia "Corrie" ten Boom, https://collections.yadvashem.org/en/righteous/4014036; Raoul Wallenberg, https://collections.yadvashem.org/en/righteous/4018150; Roddie Edmonds, https://www.yadvashem.org/righteous/stories/edmonds.html; Carol Rittner, "Denmark and the Holocaust," Shoah Resource Center, 2000, https://www.yadvashem.org/odot_pdf/Microsoft%20Word%20-%20696.pdf.

inspired and encouraged them to take up their own prophetic destinies by embracing their inheritance. That is the purpose of making Jews "jealous" and of encouraging them to go up with us to Zion to seek the Lord together.

It is true that the redemption of the nations can only happen after the Jewish nation of Israel is fully redeemed and living in their promised ancestral homeland. Those of us from the nations have an indispensable part in this process, as our fathers and mothers in the faith have shown us, as demonstrated by the faith of those who came before us and as our brothers and sisters are exemplifying today. The promised restoration of Israel is happening and will be completed exactly as God has decreed. The question is whether we will actively participate in it or remain spectators on the sidelines.

If not us, who? If not now, when?

CHAPTER 9

BECAUSE YOU ARE PART OF THE COMMONWEALTH OF ISRAEL

From what I recall of my younger years, I was the "good" child. It's not that my brother was bad or any more disobedient than I was, but I was better at playing the game of compliance. In time, thanks to the wisdom and perseverance of our godly parents, aunts and uncles, and teachers at church and school, we outgrew our childish tendencies to go our own ways. It took some time, and we experienced a measure of sibling rivalry along the way, but we did eventually grow up.

Our sibling rivalry was an important part of our growing up. We grew jealous of one another at times, particularly when it came to seeking the affections of our parents and other authority figures. Jealousy usually provoked me to compliance, but it provoked my brother to noncompliance and even rebellion. That's why I had the reputation of being the "good" child.

I can't say exactly what brought the change, but as our high school years drew to a close, we began to see the wider horizons of life and understood that God had greater purposes for us than seeking affirmation from others. That's when we began to understand and appreciate the different qualities he had built into each of us. Now, instead of feeling jealous, we look on one another with respect and admiration for the great things our Creator has done in and through us.

This is what our God has always intended for his Covenant family, as Paul explains:

> But I ask, did Israel not understand? First Moses says, "I will make you jealous of those who are not a nation; with a foolish

nation I will make you angry." Then Isaiah is so bold as to
say, "I have been found by those who did not seek me; I have
shown myself to those who did not ask for me." But of Israel
he says, "All day long I have held out my hands to a disobedient and contrary people."
—Romans 10:19-21

Paul quotes from the Song of Moses in Deuteronomy 32 and from God's indictment of Israel in Isaiah 65. These have become bywords for Christians over the centuries, but do we understand their context? Paul provides it a few verses later:

So I ask, did they stumble in order that they might fall? By no
means! Rather, through their trespass salvation has come to
the Gentiles, so as to make Israel jealous. Now if their trespass
means riches for the world, and if their failure means riches for
the Gentiles, how much more will their full inclusion mean!
Now I am speaking to you Gentiles. Inasmuch then as I am
an apostle to the Gentiles, I magnify my ministry in order
somehow to make my fellow Jews jealous, and thus save some
of them.
—Romans 11:11-14

We are conditioned to think that "making Israel jealous" means acting in a way that will cause Jewish people to accept Jesus and be saved. That's a problem when the Jesus we have preached has been divorced from his Jewish context. That's why Jewish people have resisted the Christian gospel. Jewish cultural memory, carried for centuries in the synagogues, yeshivas, and Sabbath evening prayers around the family table, remembers the same Song of Moses Paul referenced:

They have made me jealous with what is no god; they have
provoked me to anger with their idols. So I will make them
jealous with those who are no people; I will provoke them to
anger with a foolish nation.
—Deuteronomy 32:21

The persecution of Jews by Christians throughout history could be
seen as a way God allowed a "non-people" to vex, or provoke to anger,
rebellious Israel. This is why Paul warned Christians, as followers of Jesus
from the nations, not to boast about being grafted into the olive tree
of Israel in place of the branches that were broken off. He also emphasized the importance of remembering that it is the root of the tree that
supports us, not the other way around. Sadly, the church as a whole has
disregarded the apostle's counsel. That, perhaps, is part of the fulfillment
of God's discipline on his Covenant people—or at least the Jewish part.

And yet, the Jews are still here, and they are once again reborn into
a people with a nation-state on their own ancestral land. Perhaps that is
how the Jewish part of Israel's Covenant commonwealth has vexed the
non-Jewish Christian part. God did this even though many Jewish people
are secular, and observant Jews continue to cling tightly to the Torah
which Christians maintain is no longer relevant. Most Jews, regardless of
their spiritual status, continue to remain aloof to the Messianic claims of
Jesus, and yet God still blesses them. Why is that?

Perhaps Jewish observers are wondering why Christians, who dis-
regard much of the Torah, are blessed of God by expanding across the
entire world, making disciples from every tribe and tongue and nation,
and remaining true to the light they have received from the same God of
Israel whom Jews worship.

It is as if we have been talking past each other for two millennia. We each strive to do our best to serve God in the way he has revealed to us, while demeaning our siblings' service to God.

We Christians look forward to the return of our Messiah, when "they shall mourn for him, as one mourns for an only child, and weep bitterly over him, as one weeps over a firstborn." (Zechariah 12:10) We rightly interpret "they" to refer to the Jewish people in the land of Israel. What we miss is that all of us are to mourn for him whom we have pierced. That's what Amos says in his prophecy given to the northern kingdom of Israel just before the Assyrian Empire took them into captivity:

> I will turn your feasts into mourning and all your songs into
> lamentation; I will bring sackcloth on every waist and baldness
> on every head; I will make it like the mourning for an only son
> and the end of it like a bitter day.
> —Amos 8:10

That mourning happened when the northern kingdom was abolished as God had decreed. Why that mourning has any application to modern Christians is a mystery that God is revealing in our time. Put simply, it's because all of us Gentile Christians (non-Jewish believers in Jesus Christ from the nations) become part of the commonwealth of Israel by virtue of pledging allegiance to Israel's Messiah-King.

That may sound strange at first hearing, but think about it: when people invite Jesus into their hearts, or accept Jesus as Lord and Savior, what exactly are they doing? If Jesus of Nazareth really is the promised descendant of David the King of Israel who is to rule and reign over his father's realm forever, then people who accept him as Lord are acknowledging his identity as ruler of a national entity God called into existence for the purpose of bringing salvation to all peoples. That redemptive entity is called Israel. That is why Paul goes to great lengths in his epistles to explain that people who were born Gentiles take on a new identity when they profess their faith in Jesus Christ and come into his kingdom. Consider these examples:

- We are wild branches grafted into the cultivated tree of Israel (Romans 11:17-24).

- We are no longer aliens and strangers to the Commonwealth of Israel and covenants of promise, but are brought near by the blood of Christ (Ephesians 2:11-13).

- By professing allegiance to Jesus the Messiah, the son of David, the son of Abraham, we become "Abraham's offspring [seed], heirs according to the promise" (Galatians 3:29; Matthew 3:8-9; Romans 4:1-12).

- We from the nations do not replace the Jewish people in the kingdom of our God and of his Christ, but join with them to become "one new man" (Ephesians 2:14-22).

This "one new man" concept is not a statement that the church has replaced Israel. Rather, Paul builds on the writings of Moses and the prophets to make his case for the continuity and expansion of Israel. His consistent theme is that Gentiles who follow Jesus come into the commonwealth of Israel alongside Jews who remain faithful to God's calling and commandments. He and James both argue that Jews and non-Jews share Abraham as their common ancestor in the faith, even if they do not share him as a physical ancestor. James argues that all who identify as Abraham's descendants must have faith in God and demonstrate that faith by obeying God's commandments, just as Abraham did (James 2:18-26). Paul emphasizes the unity that the circumcised Jews and uncircumcised, adopted non-Jews have in Abraham:

> Is this blessing then only for the circumcised, or also for the uncircumcised? For we say that faith was counted to Abraham as righteousness. How then was it counted to him? Was it before or after he had been circumcised? It was not after, but before he was circumcised. He received the sign of circumcision as a seal of the righteousness that he had by faith while he was still uncircumcised. The purpose was to make him the father of all who believe without being circumcised, so that righteousness would be counted to them as well, and to make him the father of the circumcised who are not merely circumcised but who also walk in the footsteps of the faith that our father Abraham had before he was circumcised.
>
> —Romans 4:9-12

We Christians appreciate this connection to Abraham and even appreciate the fact that Jesus is Israel's Messiah-King, but we are not so sure about our genuine connection to Israel, particularly the part about connecting with Jewish Israelites as equal members of this commonwealth of faith in Israel's God. However, that connection is the working part of the definition of "New Covenant Christian." We take that title from what Jesus said at the Last Supper when he presented the cup to his disciples and said, "This cup that is poured out for you is the new covenant in my blood" (Luke 22:20). The terms of this New Covenant are recorded in Hebrews 8:8-12, which quotes directly from Jeremiah 31:31-34. The Hebrews passage says this:

> "Behold, the days are coming, declares the Lord, when I will establish a new covenant with the house of Israel and with the house of Judah, not like the covenant that I made with their fathers on the day when I took them by the hand to bring

them out of the land of Egypt. For they did not continue in
my covenant, and so I showed no concern for them, declares
the Lord. For this is the covenant that I will make with the
house of Israel after those days, declares the Lord: I will put my
laws into their minds, and write them on their hearts, and I
will be their God, and they shall be my people. And they shall
not teach, each one his neighbor and each one his brother,
saying, 'Know the Lord,' for they shall all know me, from the
least of them to the greatest. For I will be merciful toward their
iniquities, and I will remember their sins no more."
—Hebrews 8:8-12

The terms of the New Covenant surprised me when I first discovered
them. That happened more than three decades after I professed my faith
in Christ, when I realized that I did not know what "New Covenant
believer" means. When I looked it up, three things stood out to me:

1. That the New Covenant didn't abolish the Law, or Torah, but
   instead replaced our faulty hearts with new hearts that could
   obey God's standards of righteousness in ways our old sinful
   nature never could (see also Ezekiel 36:22-32).
2. That the New Covenant wasn't about creating some new spiritual entity called the church, but about restoring the "old covenant" entity called Israel.
3. That the New Covenant is made specifically with the house of
   Israel and the house of Judah, and that they are the component
   parts of a greater house of Israel that encompasses everyone who
   comes into this covenant. In other words, the New Covenant is
   the context in which Jews and Gentiles become "one new man."

The history of Israel since the days of Jacob's sons has been the history of the two primary divisions of the Covenant nation. The house of Judah formed around the tribe of Judah, which Jacob said would be the ruling tribe (Genesis 49:8-12). The house of Israel formed around the tribe of Joseph, and specifically around the tribe of Joseph's son Ephraim, which Jacob declared would carry the family name (Genesis 48:15-16). This family division, or sibling rivalry, provides a context for understanding how Jews and Gentiles become one new man in Christ. It also provides an explanation of the mystery by which Israel (meaning the Jews) and the church (meaning Gentile believers in Jesus) fulfill God's plan of redemption for all nations.

I like to think of it this way: I'm not Jewish, so if I am a New Covenant believer and grafted into God's Covenant nation, then I must have become part of the non-Jewish house of Israel. That perspective helps me understand why Jewish people have not, for the most part, accepted Christ in the way Christians wish they would, and yet still have a part in the Kingdom. It also helps me understand my place, which is not to usurp the inheritance of my Jewish brethren, but to help them secure and protect their inheritance so that, in the fullness of time, we may all see the final redemption of Israel and the nations. The agent that makes this possible is the blood of Christ, which activates the New Covenant and opens the way for all to come in.

This may be the most important point in how this message of New Covenant Israelite identity applies to Christian Zionism. A quick study of New Covenant passages, such as Jeremiah 31, Ezekiel 20 and 36, and Amos 9, reveals that they all speak of Israel's regathering and restoration. The case could be made that the apostles who wrote the New Testament believed that the Gentiles coming to faith in Christ were somehow the reconstituted house of Israel, and that through them God was fulfilling his promises to restore the kingdom to Israel (as they had asked Jesus just before his ascension, according to Acts 1:6-8).[1]

When the nation was divided after the death of Solomon, the rebellious tribes of the house of Israel renounced allegiance to the Davidic dynasty by refusing to accept David's grandson, Rehoboam, as their king. The biblical record says:

> And when all Israel saw that the king did not listen to them, the people answered the king, **"What portion do we have in David? We have no inheritance in the son of Jesse. To your tents, O Israel! Look now to your own house, David."** So Israel went to their tents. But Rehoboam reigned over the people of Israel who lived in the cities of Judah. Then King Rehoboam sent Adoram, who was taskmaster over the forced labor, and all Israel stoned him to death with stones. And King Rehoboam hurried to mount his chariot to flee to Jerusalem. **So Israel has been in rebellion against the house of David to this day.**
> —1 Kings 12:16-19 (emphasis added)

This may explain why Jesus emphasized his intent to go after the lost sheep of the house of Israel (Matthew 10:5-6, 15:24): they were the ones who first rejected him when they rejected the authority of his father David's house. When Christians emphasize Jesus, Son of David, above all else, they are reversing this rebellious act of their spiritual ancestors. They began as a non-people, as a community of faith taken from every nation, tribe, and tongue, and over the course of twenty centuries have

---

1   For a scholarly treatment of this topic, see Jason A. Staples, *Paul and the Resurrection of Israel: Jews, Former Gentiles, Israelites* (New York: Cambridge University Press, 2024)

been gathered into a single spiritual entity called the commonwealth of Israel, just as the prophets foretold. If the prophets are correct in this much, then we can conclude that they are also correct in the full restoration of all Israel, which is what Paul means when he describes the reality of Jews and Gentiles united under the coming reign of Messiah Son of David as "one new man."

This blessed time, which Christians call the Millennium and Jews call the Messianic Age, is a time when the sibling rivalry that has divided God's Covenant people is at last put to rest. Isaiah tells us about that in one of the most comprehensive prophecies of the Messianic Age:

> In that day the root of Jesse [Messiah, Son of David], who
> shall stand as a signal for the peoples—of him shall the nations
> inquire, and his resting place shall be glorious. In that day
> the Lord will extend his hand yet a second time to recover
> the remnant that remains of his people, from Assyria, from
> Egypt, from Pathros, from Cush, from Elam, from Shinar,
> from Hamath, and from the coastlands of the sea. He will
> raise a signal for the nations and will assemble the banished of
> Israel, and gather the dispersed of Judah from the four corners
> of the earth. The jealousy of Ephraim [Israel] shall depart, and
> those who harass Judah shall be cut off; **Ephraim shall not be
> jealous of Judah, and Judah shall not harass Ephraim.** But
> they shall swoop down on the shoulder of the Philistines in the
> west, and together they shall plunder the people of the east.
> They shall put out their hand against Edom and Moab, and
> the Ammonites shall obey them.
> —Isaiah 11:10-14 (emphasis added)

This has not yet happened. The world is now witnessing the regathering and restoration of Judah, the Jewish part of God's Covenant people. There is not yet an Ephraim or house of Israel existing as such, but multitudes from the nations have pledged their allegiance to the Messiah-King of Israel and have been adopted into the nation God created as the vehicle of redemption for all nations.

These are the people of Israel whom God called "not my people." They have come back to life through the spiritual descendants redeemed by the Messiah God sent into the world to bring back the lost sheep of the house of Israel. He has turned our mourning into dancing, just as he is turning the mourning of our Jewish siblings into dancing. It's still a mystery how this is happening, but we know that Messiah is the agent who makes it happen. We also know that one day, after we have finished making each other jealous, we will rejoice together in his presence.

CHAPTER 10

BECAUSE THE ALTERNATIVE IS UNTHINKABLE

Popular movements are most effective when the people attending the rallies, marches, and other events understand the issues they are addressing. In the United States, movements for women's suffrage, labor unions, civil rights, feminism, and the right to life have been effective because those issues impacted both supporters and opponents on a deep level. Each of those movements made use of slogans and catchphrases to summarize their cause and generate enthusiasm. That's why phrases like "Votes for women," "A fair day's wage for a fair day's work," "Power to the people," "Women's rights are human rights," and "A person's a person, no matter how small" remain memorable and impactful.

Those slogans made sense because the people who used them believed them and put their beliefs into action. They might not have been able to argue the nuances of their movements, but they understood on a personal level what the movement meant to them. These were their stories—the stories of the disenfranchised half of America, the exploited workers, the marginalized African American citizens, the marginalized women of all segments of society, and the unborn and those who cherish them.

What, then, are we to think of movements in which the masses have little understanding of the issues and have little or no personal stake in the cause? What if the slogans they use are simply words repeated without question? Is such a movement truly a popular movement? Can it be effective in achieving lasting change for good or for ill?

This is why we have to ask what pro-Palestinian protesters mean when they chant, "From the river to the sea, Palestine will be free!"

Protests calling for the liberation of Arab Palestine erupted all over the world in the wake of the Hamas massacres of Israeli civilians on October 7, 2023. The protests escalated as Israel responded with military force to neutralize the existential threat from Hamas in Gaza, Hezbollah in Lebanon, Arab Palestinian terrorism in Judea and Samaria, and Iranian-led missile and drone attacks from Yemen, Syria, Iraq, and Iran itself. Videos abound of anti-Israel and anti-Jewish protests in London, New York, Sydney, Paris, Los Angeles, and many other cities. It did not help that the media outlets and the governments of the world parroted without question the baseless Hamas propaganda accusing Israel of genocide.

In an age when social media influences the hearts and minds of billions, carefully staged and AI-generated images of supposedly dead or injured children are guaranteed to elicit the desired response from those who, until recently, had probably never given a moment's thought to the Arab-Israeli conflict and the justice—or lack thereof—of the Palestinian Arab cause. What the protesters have forgotten, or perhaps never knew, is that Jews and Arabs living under the British Mandatory Government in Palestine were both called Palestinians. It was only after Israel's independence in 1948 that Jewish Palestinians began to be called Israelis, and the term Palestinian began to be applied solely to Arabs living in the western portion of the former Mandatory territory. Hence the amusing video clips on social media of people who could not answer coherently what they mean in their demands for Palestine to be free from the river to the sea. If the issue were truly important to them, they might at least look at a map to learn which river and which sea.[1]

---

1   Two examples of responses from protesters in New York and London when asked what "From the river to the sea" means are Carter, Sara and Sean Hannity, "Anti-Israel protesters can't seem to define 'from the river to the sea,'" Fox News, April 24,

The river, of course, is the Jordan River, and the sea is the Mediterranean. What the Arab Palestinian activists want, and what their non-Arab, non-Muslim supporters are yelling about, is the destruction of the world's only Jewish State so that an Arab Muslim Palestinian state can be established in its place. This is not about "land for peace," as seen in historical agreements like the 1979 Camp David Accords, where Israel returned the Sinai Peninsula to Egypt in exchange for peace (see Map 9, Israel After Peace with Egypt, March 26, 1979). It happened again in 1993 when Israel and the Palestinian Liberation Organization (PLO) signed the Oslo Accords, in which the PLO became the Palestinian Authority (PA) and agreed to share control over Judea and Samaria. Another example was in 2005, when Israel unilaterally withdrew from Gaza, transferring its administration to the PA.

This is also not about a two-state solution, such as was offered to the Arab Palestinians in 1937 (Peel Commission), 1947 (United Nations Partition Plan), 1993 (Oslo Accords), 2000 (Camp David Summit), and 2020 (Trump Deal of the Century). If the Arabs truly wanted a Palestinian state (other than the Kingdom of Jordan, which was established in the eastern portion of British Mandatory Palestine in 1921), then they could have had it at just about any point in the last century and likely

---

2024, news video, 3:02, https://youtu.be/Lx8PQ5ktQPE?si=QwNvacTLcg2HYJ8Q; and Kistin, Konstantin, "Asking Palestine Protestors What From the River to the Sea Means," Triggernometry, April 20, 2024, educational video, 5:32, https://youtu.be/z-AmRRb84Us?si=N313572KW2oQZMT0. For a humorous and informed editorial view of the Israel-Hamas conflict, see Maher, Bill, "New Rule: From the River to the Sea | Real Time with Bill Maher (HBO)," Real Time with Bill Maher, December 15, 2023, entertainment video, 8:12 https://youtu.be/KP-CRXROorw?si=0gZTwHY8KvZcrSAk. Maher points out how the slogan, "From the river to the sea Palestine will be free," is not only antisemitic, but genocidal. For an Israeli view using humor to make the same point, see Dani, "Israel Vs. Hamas: From the river to the sea?" AskDani, educational video, November 2, 2023, 2:20, https://youtu.be/Uwvd7xGQV10?si=ypAZ8lCchRmyuPC9.

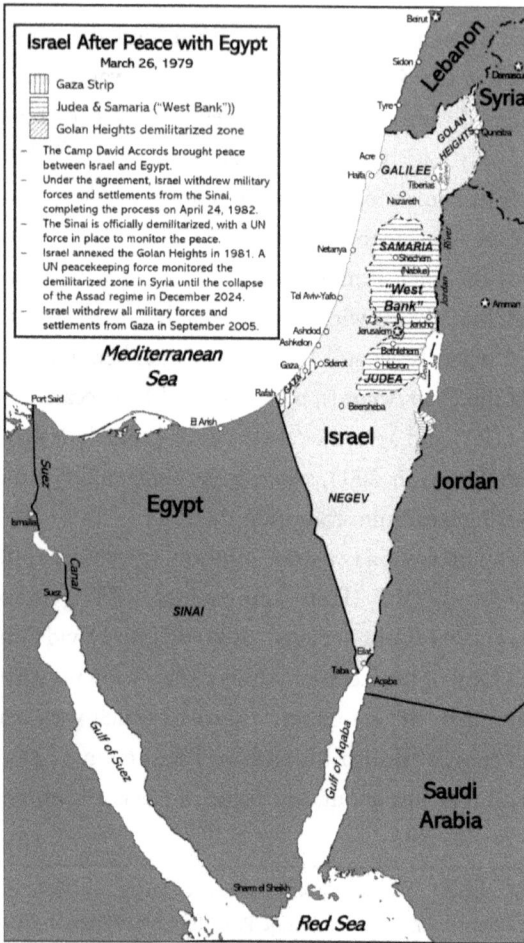

Israel After Peace with Egypt
March 26, 1979

- Gaza Strip
- Judea & Samaria ("West Bank"))
- Golan Heights demilitarized zone

- The Camp David Accords brought peace between Israel and Egypt.
- Under the agreement, Israel withdrew military forces and settlements from the Sinai, completing the process on April 24, 1982.
- The Sinai is officially demilitarized, with a UN force in place to monitor the peace.
- Israel annexed the Golan Heights in 1981. A UN peacekeeping force monitored the demilitarized zone in Syria until the collapse of the Assad regime in December 2024.
- Israel withdrew all military forces and settlements from Gaza in September 2005.

Map 9. Israel After Peace with Egypt, March 26, 1979. (Based on Public Domain Map by Honza Havlíček, derived from 1967_Six_Day_War_-_Battle_of_Golan_Heights.jpg: Mr. Edward J. Krasnoborski and Mr. Frank Martini, Department of History, U.S. Military Academy, via Wikimedia Commons, https:// commons.wikimedia.org/wiki/File:Israel_1949-1967.svg; Israel_and_surroundings_location_map.svg: NordNordWestEgypt_location_map.svg: NordNordWestLebanon_location_map.svg: NordNordWest deriva- tive work: Mapeh, CC BY-SA 3.0 https://creativecommons.org/licenses/by-sa/3.0, via Wikimedia Commons, https://upload.wikimedia.org/wikipedia/commons/6/65/Israel_and_surroundings_location_map.svg.)

would have enjoyed Jewish Israeli partnership in making both states prosperous and secure.

But it's not about peaceful coexistence. It's about the total elimination of the Jewish State and returning any surviving Jews to the oppressive status they endured in Islamic regimes prior to the establishment of Israel. That has been the stated goal of the PLO since its establishment in 1964. The revised PLO Charter of 1968, which was never revoked even after the PLO agreed to the Oslo Accords, explicitly calls for the destruction of Israel in language like this:

ARTICLE 19: The partitioning of Palestine in 1947 and the establishment of Israel is fundamentally null and void, whatever time has elapsed. . . .

ARTICLE 20: The Balfour Declaration, the Mandate Document, and what has been based upon them are considered null and void. The claim of a historical or spiritual tie between Jews and Palestine does not tally with historical realities nor with the constituents of statehood in their true sense. Judaism, in its character as a religion of revelation, is not a nationality with an independent existence. Likewise, the Jews are not one people with an independent personality. They are rather citizens of the states to which they belong.

ARTICLE 21: The Palestinian Arab people, in expressing itself through the armed Palestinian revolution, rejects every solution that is a substitute for a complete liberation of Palestine, and rejects all plans that aim at the settlement of the Palestine issue or its internationalization.

> ARTICLE 22: Israel is a constant threat to peace in the Middle
> East and the entire world. Since the liberation of Palestine will
> liquidate the Zionist and imperialist presence and bring about
> the stabilization of peace in the Middle East, the people of
> Palestine looks to the support of liberal men of the world and
> all the forces of good progress and peace...[2]

This is not the language of an organization advocating national self-determination in the sense Woodrow Wilson intended with his Fourteen Points, nor as people in Western Democracies understand it. Rather, as Benjamin Netanyahu notes, "So long as it has not formally been repealed by the Palestinian National Council, the charter stands as compelling proof that the basic Palestinian grievance against Israel remains existential and not merely territorial."[3]

This is the position of the "moderate" Palestinian Authority, the organization trusted with the responsibility of shepherding into existence an Arab state that would exist peacefully next to Israel. The masquerade worked for a time, but in the aftermath of October 7th, even former US President Bill Clinton, the man who brokered the 1993 Oslo Accords, admitted that PLO leader Yassir Arafat had deceived him and never intended to honor the agreement.[4]

Since the "moderate" and "secular" PA takes this approach to the existence of Israel, it should be no surprise that the more Islamist

2   Palestine Liberation Organization: The Palestine National Charter (July 17, 1968), *Jewish Virtual Library*, https://www.jewishvirtuallibrary.org/the-palestine-national-charter-july-1968.

3   Netanyahu, *A Durable Peace*, 203.

4   Yishai Fleisher, "Muslim Crowd GOES SILENT as Bill Clinton reveals the WHOLE Truth about Israel 'Palestine,'" *Yishai Fleisher*, November 3, 2024, editorial video, 22:36, https://youtu.be/nXu-rS-W-6E?si=2ck1S2MsR8WY3zGK.

and militant Islamic Resistance Movement, or Hamas, takes the same approach. If anything, the Hamas Charter of 1988 is even more extreme than the PLO Charter in that it incorporates references from the Quran and other Islamic texts, as well as the thoroughly discredited *Protocols of the Elders of Zion*, the "most widely distributed antisemitic publication of modern times."[5] According to the Hamas Charter:

> ARTICLE 7: The Islamic Resistance Movement is one link in the chain of jihad in confronting the Zionist invasion. . . the Islamic Resistance Movement aspires to realize the promise of Allah, no matter how long it takes. The Prophet [Muhammad], Allah's prayer and peace be upon him, says: "The hour of judgment shall not come until the Muslims fight the Jews and kill them, so that the Jews hide behind trees and stones, and each tree and stone will say: 'Oh Muslim, oh servant of Allah, there is a Jew behind me, come and kill him'. . . ."

> ARTICLE ELEVEN: The Islamic Resistance Movement maintains that the land of Palestine is Waqf [Islamic religious endowment] land given as endowment for all generations of Muslims until the Day of Resurrection. One should not neglect it or [even] a part of it, nor should one relinquish it

---

5   Since its publication in Russia in 1903, the fictitious *Protocols of the Elders of Zion* has been used by antisemites to justify their anti-Jewish ideology. Adolf Hitler and Hajj Amin al-Husayni, for example, pointed to the *Protocols* as proof of a supposed Jewish plot to take over the world. Although exposed as a fraud in 1921, the *Protocols* continue to influence the anti-Jewish conspiracy theories and blood libels of Islamists, white supremacists, neo-Nazis, and other antisemites. "Protocols of the Elders of Zion," *Holocaust Encyclopedia*, United States Holocaust Memorial Museum, https://encyclopedia.ushmm.org/content/en/article/protocols-of-the-elders-of-zion.

or [even] a part of it. . . This is the legal status of the land of Palestine according to Islamic law. In this respect, it is like any other land that the Muslims have conquered by force, because the Muslims consecrated it at the time of the conquest as religious endowment for all generations of Muslims until the Day of Resurrection.

ARTICLE THIRTEEN: The initiatives, the so-called peace solutions, and the international conferences for resolving the Palestinian problem stand in contradiction to the principles of the Islamic Resistance Movement, for to neglect any part of Palestine is to neglect part of the Islamic faith. The nationalism of the Islamic Resistance Movement is part of its [Islamic] faith. It is in the light of this principle that its members are educated, and they wage jihad in order to raise the banner of Allah over the homeland...

ARTICLE TWENTY-SEVEN: The Palestine Liberation Organization [PLO] is closest to the heart of the Islamic Resistance Movement. [We regard it as] a father, brother or friend, and a true Muslim does not spurn his father, his brother or his friend. Our homeland is one, our misfortune is one, our destiny is one and we share the same enemy.

ARTICLE THIRTY-TWO: In the circle of the conflict against world Zionism, the Islamic Resistance Movement sees itself as a spearhead or as a step forward on the road [to victory]. It joins its efforts to the efforts of all those who are active in the Palestinian arena. It now remains for steps to be taken by the Arab and Islamic world. [The Islamic Resistance Movement] is

well qualified for the upcoming stage [of the struggle] with the
Jews, the warmongers.[6]

These are the positions of just two of Israel's enemies. The same
intent to eliminate the Jewish State is summarized in the rhetoric of the
Islamic Republic of Iran, which refers to the "Zionist entity" of Israel
as the "Little Satan" that must be resisted and destroyed in the struggle
against Zionism and Western imperialism.

If Israel is the "Little Satan," then there must be a "Great Satan" prop-
ping up the Zionist entity and leading the imperialist global order. That,
of course, is the United States. The Iranian regime, which remains true
to the revolutionary principles of its founder, Ayatollah Ruhollah Kho-
meini, has been attempting not only to establish a new order based on
Iranian Shi'a Islam, but also to be recognized as the leader of all branches
of Islam in this struggle against the existing world order. Current Iranian
Supreme Leader Ayatollah Seyyed Ali Hosseini Khamenei is continuing
in that effort, as one journalist explains:

> The ayatollah's reign of terror is driven by a mix of geopolitical,
> ideological, and security objectives. They are: To destroy and
> eliminate the state of Israel and oppose Western imperialism;
> to establish Iran as the leader of the global Shi'ite community
> and the broader Islamic world; to export Shi'ism to the Middle
> East and beyond; for Iran to become the dominant power
> in the [Persian] Gulf; for Iran to be a nuclear power, thereby

---

6   The Hamas Charter, August 18, 1988, Menahem Milson, trans. In "The Hamas Charter
     – The Ideology Behind The Massacre," MEMRI Special Dispatch No. 10897, The Middle
     East Media Research Institute (MEMRI), October 23, 2023, https://www.memri.org/
     reports/hamas-charter-%E2%80%93-ideology-behind-massacre.

enabling her to project power worldwide; to upend the rules-based, free market, democratic system that was established by the United States and replace it with a world order that forwards the Iranian agenda. This is done in tandem with Russia, China, and North Korea.[7]

What many in the West fail to grasp is that the war against the Jewish state is also a war against the Jewish people, their values, and the foundations of Western civilization rooted in Judeo-Christian principles. We should ask ourselves: What would happen if the enemies of the Jewish people and the Jewish state succeed in destroying both? Why would we suppose that the horrific actions of the demonically-inspired terrorists on October 7th wouldn't inspire hordes of others around the globe to follow suit? If Israel ceases to exist, what would prevent those who call for the destruction of both the Jewish people and the West from following through on their threats? And who could defend against them without the spiritual, moral, and civilizational foundation we have inherited from the Jews?

British journalist Douglas Murray is not optimistic that the West can survive if there is no Israel, as he explained in an interview with Ben Shapiro:

> This is one of the underpinnings of Western Civilization utterly, utterly at risk – and not in a sort of metaphorical way . . . How many Jews are there in the world? 15 million. . . There are lots of conflicts in the world, and I've covered a lot of conflicts involving a lot of people, but it's conceivable that

---

7   Andrew J. Masigan, "The Ayatollah's Reign Of Terror," MEMRI Daily Brief No. 665, October 28, 2024, https://www.memri.org/reports/ayatollahs-reign-terror.

at some point 15 million Christians could be killed. It would be a disaster, a tragedy. It's conceivable that at some point in Burma or India some 15 million Muslims could be killed. It would be a disaster. It would be a tragedy of an unimaginable scale – of mid-20th century scale. But if 15 million Jews were killed, that's the end of the story. That's it. Now what does that mean for the Jewish people? [It means] that the people who saw off everyone from Pharaoh to Hitler [would have] disappeared in the 21st century. Everyone else in my view wouldn't survive either. Western Civilization could not survive the destruction of the Jewish State because it would be among much else the cutting away of the whole tree that we're on and Western Civilization would die.[8]

Murray's remarks echo Paul's exhortation that we from the nations do not support the root of Israel's olive tree. On the contrary, the root supports us (Romans 11:17-18). He is right, of course—we cannot survive for long in a world where there is no Israel, no synagogues, no Torah studies, and no Jewish communities reminding us by their very presence that there is a God who governs the affairs of mankind. Like Tolkien's Middle Earth after the departure of the Elves, all that they had breathed into existence and nurtured would fade away into the stuff of memory, and the promises of God to restore, revive, and redeem his chosen people would fall to the dust.

This is the unthinkable alternative: the discrediting of the God of the Universe. It's the same unthinkable alternative that prompted Moses

---

8   Douglas Murray, "Our Last Chance to Save the West," *The Ben Shapiro Show Sunday Special*, July 7, 2024, educational video, 1:20:46 (excerpt from 27:10-31:23), https://youtu.be/P5F0q6LPnT4?si=Yy6EenY35GQrUIaA.

to reason with the Almighty after the ancient Israelites fell into sin with their Golden Calf idol:

> And the LORD said to Moses, "I have seen this people, and behold, it is a stiff-necked people. Now therefore let me alone, that my wrath may burn hot against them and I may consume them, in order that I may make a great nation of you." But Moses implored the LORD his God and said, "O LORD, why does your wrath burn hot against your people, whom you have brought out of the land of Egypt with great power and with a mighty hand? Why should the Egyptians say, 'With evil intent did he bring them out, to kill them in the mountains and to consume them from the face of the earth'? Turn from your burning anger and relent from this disaster against your people. Remember Abraham, Isaac, and Israel, your servants, to whom you swore by your own self, and said to them, 'I will multiply your offspring as the stars of heaven, and all this land that I have promised I will give to your offspring, and they shall inherit it forever.'" And the LORD relented from the disaster that he had spoken of bringing on his people.
> —Exodus 32:9-14

This is the certainty we have that the God of Israel will not allow his people to be destroyed. It never has been about them—it's about *him*. He said as much to Ezekiel when he was on the verge of allowing the last independent Israelite kingdom to be conquered by the Babylonians:

> "As for you, O house of Israel, thus says the Lord GOD: Go serve every one of you his idols, now and hereafter, if you will not listen to me; **but my holy name you shall no more**

profane with your gifts and your idols. "For on my holy mountain, the mountain height of Israel, declares the Lord GOD, there all the house of Israel, all of them, shall serve me in the land. There I will accept them, and there I will require your contributions and the choicest of your gifts, with all your sacred offerings. As a pleasing aroma I will accept you, when I bring you out from the peoples and gather you out of the countries where you have been scattered. And I will manifest my holiness among you in the sight of the nations. And you shall know that I am the LORD, when I bring you into the land of Israel, the country that I swore to give to your fathers. And there you shall remember your ways and all your deeds with which you have defiled yourselves, and you shall loathe yourselves for all the evils that you have committed. And you shall know that I am the LORD, **when I deal with you for my name's sake**, not according to your evil ways, nor according to your corrupt deeds, O house of Israel, declares the Lord GOD."

—Ezekiel 20:39-44 (emphasis added)

God's plan for the redemption of the whole world cannot be completed without Israel because the key component of that plan is the promise of redemption he made to Abraham, Isaac, and Jacob, the Patriarchs of Israel. That is what inspired Paul to write the following:

Then what advantage has the Jew? Or what is the value of circumcision? Much in every way. To begin with, the Jews were entrusted with the oracles of God. What if some were unfaithful? Does their faithlessness nullify the faithfulness of God? By

no means! Let God be true though every one were a liar, as it is written, "That you may be justified in your words, and prevail when you are judged."
—Romans 3:1-4

The outcome is certain: God will fulfill his plan, bringing salvation to the Jewish people and to all who attach themselves to the commonwealth of Israel. The real question is who will respond to God's call to serve as his agents in the restoration and final redemption of Israel.

God will never allow Israel's destruction, nor the permanent shaming of his name. This leaves us but one more unthinkable alternative: that those he intends to bless for supporting Israel might turn away from that blessing—and potentially step into a curse.

CONCLUSION

RESTORING THE
FORTUNES OF ZION

Sometimes passages in the Bible suddenly come to life with new meaning. That often happens because we experience something that sheds new light on those passages, making them more relevant to us. That happened to me with this familiar psalm:

> When the LORD restored the fortunes of Zion, we were like those who dream. Then our mouth was filled with laughter, and our tongue with shouts of joy; then they said among the nations, "The LORD has done great things for them." The LORD has done great things for us; we are glad.
> —Psalm 126:1-3

The relevance of Psalm 126 dawned on me at The Israel Summit in Franklin, Tennessee, in May 2024. That groundbreaking conference brought together hundreds of Christian and Jewish Zionists to express our mutual support for Israel in the existential crisis of the war with Hamas and the global outpouring of antisemitism sparked by that war. At the end of the gathering, one of the Jewish speakers presented an inspirational teaching on Psalm 126, making the point that it was being fulfilled in our day, and even in the very room where we were gathered. He then invited everyone to join him in a prophetic declaration based on the psalm.

As our Jewish friends gathered on the stage, all of us from the nations (Gentiles) stood and said to them, "The Lord has done great things for you!"

Our Jewish counterparts responded, "The Lord has done great things for us!"

We made this antiphonal declaration three times with growing enthusiasm. It was a profound spiritual moment as we realized we were declaring what God had decreed long ago and was bringing to pass the regathering of his Chosen People to the Promised Land, the rebirth of Israel, and the defeat of Israel's enemies.

What we declared in that conference room in Tennessee is a preview of what the whole world will say to the people of Israel as this process of restoration and final redemption moves toward completion. At that time, the world will see, just as we are now seeing, that God has done what he promised:

> Therefore, thus says the LORD, I have returned to Jerusalem with mercy; my house shall be built in it, declares the LORD of hosts, and the measuring line shall be stretched out over Jerusalem. Cry out again, Thus says the LORD of hosts: My cities shall again overflow with prosperity, and the LORD will again comfort Zion and again choose Jerusalem.
> —Zechariah 1:16-17

These promises come immediately after a declaration God makes about Zion and about the nations that count themselves as Zion's enemies:

> Thus says the LORD of hosts: I am exceedingly jealous for Jerusalem and for Zion. And I am exceedingly angry with the nations that are at ease; for while I was angry but a little, they furthered the disaster.
> —Zechariah 1:14-15

God's declaration may come as an unpleasant surprise to the leaders of Iran and other enemies of Israel who refer to the Jewish State as "the Zionist entity." Their reference is misplaced. Israel is not the Zionist entity—God is.

Jesus asked his disciples whether the Son of Man would find faith in the earth when he comes (Luke 18:8). We Christians have labored for centuries to answer that question by doing the works he did. Until this generation, we had little understanding that those works would include helping the Jewish people return home and receive the inheritance promised to them. Now we know that Jesus intended this all along because it is what his Father intended all along. Perhaps these two thousand years of Christian history have been the story of God preparing a people to join with his Chosen People to prepare the way for the final revelation of Messiah that we all long to see.

At the beginning of this book, I issued an invitation to you, dear reader. I ask again: Will you answer the call and join your Christian Zionist brothers and sisters in making God's redemptive plans for Israel and the nations a reality in our time? If so, consider these practical steps:

1. **Study your Bible.** Learn what God says, from Genesis to Revelation, about his land and people of Israel. With this biblical understanding, you will be equipped to recognize the lies and half-truths of those who oppose God's redemptive plans.

2. **Get to know Jewish people.** Visit a synagogue. Interact on a personal level with your Jewish neighbors and business associates. They may not be Torah scholars or even religious, but their identity as part of God's ancient Hebrew people still shapes their worldview and the direction of their lives.

3. **Investigate Jewish Bible teaching.** Jewish scholars have studied, discussed, argued over, and commented on the Torah for millennia. Jesus and the apostles drew on that same body of

ancient biblical learning to develop their teachings. This is what is meant by the Jewish roots of our faith.

4. **Learn the story of Israel.** Get to know the history of the Jewish people and the miraculous work God has done in bringing them back to the land of Israel.

5. **Go to Israel.** See how God's promises to the Jewish people and to the land itself are being fulfilled. Go once as a tourist, and after that, go as a volunteer.

And above all...

Pray for the peace of Jerusalem! May they be secure who love you!
—Psalm 122:6

APPENDIX

RESOURCES FOR
LEARNING AND ACTION

The ministries, institutions, books, movies, and news sources listed here are those that have helped me in my Christian Zionist journey. This list is intended to help those inspired to learn more about Israel, the Jewish people, and Christian involvement in the Zionist dream. These resources are Christian, Messianic Jewish, Orthodox Jewish, and secular, with considerable diversity among them, especially when it comes to theology and politics. The unifying factor is appreciation for the Jewish people and the world's only Jewish State in the ancestral homeland of the Jewish people. That is the Zionist dream as it has become reality.

This list begins with works of fiction and includes popular feature films. Fiction often conveys concepts more effectively than non-fiction. The works on this list convey aspects of Jewish history and culture that take on new meaning when viewed through a Zionist lens. For example, the antics of Mel Brooks in his comedy-drama, *To Be Or Not To Be,* portray the terror of Polish Jews and others targeted by the Holocaust in a way that a viewer new to the subject might more easily receive. Brooks' comedy serves as an entry point and a way marker for a far more serious (and traumatic) depiction of the Holocaust in Escape from Sobibor. Those who absorb the lessons of that film are ready to see how survivors of the Holocaust literally rose from the ashes to create a new reality in Eretz Israel (the Land of Israel), as depicted in *Exodus* and *Cast A Giant Shadow.*

These Hollywood versions of Israel's miraculous rebirth inspire the viewer to learn about Israel's history through the nonfiction works of Theodor Herzl, Elie Wiesel, Viktor Frankl, Benjamin Netanyahu, and David Friedman. Having then acquired a better understanding of Zionism, the student is equipped to evaluate current events through the news sources presented here, and compare them to the less-than-favorable view of Zionism and the Jewish State presented in other news and social media outlets. In time, the well-informed Christian Zionist is ready to engage in advocacy for Israel, and take action through the opportunities included among these resources.

The books listed here are available through retail sources and libraries. The links are included to provide more information on specific authors and/or the ministries associated with them. In some cases, the books can be purchased through those sites, or downloaded for free in the case of the eBook version of Herzl's *The Jewish State*.

Books (Fiction)

Arranged in chronological order of the subject matter.

- *Ahoti: A Story of Tamar* by Miriam Feinberg Vamosh and Eva Marie Everson (Brewster, MA: Paraclete Press, 2024). Based on the life of King David's daughter, Tamar, who was ravaged by her brother Amnon (2 Samuel 13), Vamosh draws on Jewish history and folklore to carry Tamar's story forward to her redemption. Visit the author's website at https://miriamfeinbergvamosh.com/.

- *The Scroll* by Miriam Feinberg Vamosh (Jerusalem: Toby Press Ltd, 2019). This novel about the survivors of the last stand of Jewish rebels at Masada as they rebuild their lives in the aftermath of Rome's victory sheds light on a critical era when Jews and Christians adjust to the new realities created by the destruction of the Temple and the end of Judean independence. Visit the author's website at https://miriamfeinbergvamosh.com/.

- *Mila 18* by Leon Uris (New York: Doubleday & Co, 1961). Novel based on the April 1943 Jewish uprising against Nazi genocide in the ghetto of Warsaw, Poland.
- *Exodus* by Leon Uris (New York: Doubleday & Co, 1958). A novel about the rebirth of Israel in 1948, as seen through the eyes of an American nurse and a Jewish freedom fighter.
- *Mitla Pass* by Leon Uris (New York: Doubleday & Co, 1988). A semi-autobiographical work that tells the story of the 1956 Sinai War through the eyes of an American writer who comes to Israel to research a new novel and finds himself caught up in the combat action.
- *QB VII* by Leon Uris (New York: Doubleday & Co, 1971). When a Jewish author whose book on the Holocaust exposes the complicity of a prominent surgeon in the Nazi death camps, the surgeon sues for libel, setting the stage for a moving courtroom drama.
- *The Master of Return and the Eleventh Light* by Adam Eliyahu Berkowitz (Jerusalem: Root Source Press, 2022). This novel based on the author's story as a Jewish pioneer in Judea explores the world of religious Jews inspired to reclaim the land of their inheritance in the face of terrorism from hostile Arab neighbors, international pressure, and challenges to their faith. Berkowitz presents Jewish settlers as they are, not as the "obstacles to peace" the world thinks they are. Available at https://root-source.com/product/the-master-of-return/.

Books (Non-Fiction)

Arranged by date of original publication.

- *The Jewish State (Der Judenstaat)* by Theodor Herzl (New York: American Zionist Emergency Council, 1946). Originally published in Vienna in 1896, Herzl's work translated the Zionist dream into a plan of action that led to the independence of Israel just 52 years later. This edition of *The Jewish State* is available at https://www.gutenberg.org/ebooks/25282.

- *Man's Search for Meaning* by Viktor Frankl (Boston: Beacon Press, 2006). First published in Vienna in 1946, this is Frankl's story of his ordeal in the death camps during the Holocaust. The trials he faced gave depth and refinement to the theory of psychology he had begun to investigate before World War II, and launched his career as a world-renowned psychologist.
- *Night* by Elie Wiesel (New York: Hill & Wang, 2006), Originally published in 1956, this is Elie Wiesel's memoir of survival as a teenager in the Nazi death camps. This famous work exposes the depth and breadth of human cruelty as Wiesel experienced it, and takes the reader on an existential journey to comprehend what the Holocaust was and what it means for us today.
- *The Hiding Place: The Triumphant True Story of Corrie Ten Boom* by Corrie Ten Boom, with John and Elizabeth Sherrill (Grand Rapids, MI: 2006). Originally published in 1971, this is the story of Corrie Ten Boom and her family as they risked everything to protect Jews in Nazi-occupied Holland. To learn more, visit the Corrie Ten Boom House at https://www.corrietenboom.com/en/home.
- *A Durable Peace: Israel and Its Place Among the Nations* by Benjamin Netanyahu (New York: Warner Books, 2000). This revised edition of Netanyahu's work originally published in 1993 traces the history of Zionism and offers a framework for lasting peace in the Middle East. Netanyahu thoroughly doc-

uments Israel's story, and the twisting of that story by those who opposed the Zionist dream and the Jewish State since before its inception.

- *The Messianic Church Arising!* by Dr. Robert Heidler (Denton, TX: Glory of Zion International, 2006). An introduction to the Jewish, or Hebraic, roots of the Christian faith, explaining how the feasts of the Jewish calendar are covenants with God, and how they belong to believers in Christ as well. Available through Glory of Zion at https://store.gloryofzion. org/products/the-messianic-church-arising?_pos=1&_ sid=6e4449d44&_ss=r

- *The LIST: Persecution of Jews by Christians Throughout History* by Bob O'Dell and Ray Montgomery (Jerusalem: Root Source Press, 2019). Christians should be aware of events like the Holocaust and the Spanish Inquisition, when people who claimed to be Christians took part in institutionalized, genocidal persecution of the Jewish people. These infamous eras grew out of a prevailing anti-Jewish attitude that can be traced to the replacement theology of the early Church Fathers. It is a sensitive and uncomfortable topic, but necessary to address in order to heal the breach between these two halves of God's Covenant People. The LIST is available from Root Source at https://root-source.com/product/the-list-per-secution-of-jews/.

- *Five Years With Orthodox Jews: How Connecting With God's People Unlocks Understanding of God's Word* by Bob O'Dell, with Gidon Ariel (Jerusalem: Root Source Press, 2020). Bob O'Dell, a Christian, already had decades of experience with Jewish colleagues in Israel as an entrepreneur when he had opportunity to partner with Gidon Ariel, an Orthodox Jew, to establish Root Source as a forum for Christians and Jews to learn from one another. In this volume, Bob shares many of the lessons he has learned from his Jewish friends and colleagues, with Gidon providing a Jewish perspective on Bob's insights. This is a unique resource for those who want to know what Christians and Jews have in common, and why they see things differently in the scriptures they both revere. Available from Root Source at https://root-source.com/product/five-years-with-orthodox-jews/.

- *Zionism and The Black Church: Why Standing with Israel Will be a Defining Issue for Christians of Color in the 21st Century*, by Dumisani Washington (Umndeni Press, 2021). A discussion of Africa's ancient connection to Israel and the Jewish people, and the historic Black-Jewish synergy in America. An explanation of the foundation of spiritual Zionism among Black people, and why that foundation will always inform Black support for Israel. Zionism and the Black Church is available from Umndeni Press at https://www.umndenipress.com/.

- *Facing Jerusalem: God's Plan for Global Redemption* by Zac Waller and Luke Hilton (Bloomington, IN: WestBow Press, 2021). After many years of experience in Israel, Zac Waller and Luke Hilton understand the importance of Jerusalem as the center of the world. It is the only city God calls his own. Why, then, do Christians not recognize the centrality of Jerusalem and Israel to our faith? Facing Jerusalem is available from The Israel Guys at https://theisraelguys.store/products/facing-jerusalem

- *Your Sabbath Invitation: Partnership in God's Ultimate Celebration* by David R. Nekrutman (Powder Springs, GA:

2022). Jewish author David Nekrutman explains how God has invited all people to join in observance of the Sabbath. He draws inspiration from Isaiah 66:23, "From new moon to new moon, and from Sabbath to Sabbath, all flesh shall come to worship before me, declares the LORD." As the only Orthodox Jew (so far) who has earned a graduate degree from a Christian university, David is uniquely equipped to present this subject in language Christians can understand and appreciate. Your Sabbath Invitation is available from https://www. yoursabbathinvitation.com/.

- *One Jewish State: The Last, Best hope to Resolve the Israeli-Palestinian Conflict* by David Friedman (West Palm Beach, FL: Humanix Books, 2024). As former US Ambassador to Israel, and as a practicing Orthodox Jew, David Friedman is well qualified to write about lasting peace in the Middle East. In *One Jewish State*, he presents a realistic alternative to the failed two-state solution that has brought endless conflict instead of peace to the Middle East.

Feature Films
Arranged in chronological order of the subject matter.

- *Fiddler on the Roof.* 1971 musical drama starring Topol, Norma Crane, and Leonard Frey. Set in pre-revolutionary Russia in 1905, a Jewish peasant with traditional values copes with marrying off three of his daughters with modern romantic ideals while growing antisemitic sentiment threatens his village.
- *Bonhoeffer: Pastor. Spy. Assassin.* 2024 historical drama starring Jonas Dassler portraying the life and career of German pastor Dietrich Bonhoeffer, who spoke out against the Nazification

of Germany and the German church, collaborated with the German resistance movement to save Jews from genocide, and was complicit in plots to assassinate Adolf Hitler.

- *To Be Or Not To Be.* 1983 comedic drama starring Mel Brooks, Anne Bancroft, and Ronny Graham. At the beginning of World War II, the German occupation of Warsaw moves a Polish actor to collaborate with the Resistance to help his theatre troupe and many others evade the Nazis and escape Poland.
- *Escape from Sobibor.* 1987 drama based on actual events, starring Alan Arkin, Joanna Pacula, and Rutger Hauer. The German death camp in Sobibor, Poland, killed two hundred fifty thousand Jews until it was shut down after a successful mass prisoner escape on October 14, 1943.
- *The Hiding Place.* 1975 drama based on actual events, starring Julie Harris, Jeannette Clift, and Arthur O'Connell. In the Netherlands during World War II, the Ten Boom family risks everything to hide Jews from the Nazis.
- *Exodus.* 1960 drama starring Paul Newman, Eva Marie Saint, and Ralph Richardson. Based on the novel by Leon Uris, the film depicts the creation of the State of Israel and the subsequent War of Independence in 1948.
- *Cast A Giant Shadow.* 1966 drama starring Kirk Douglas, John Wayne, and Frank Sinatra. In 1947, following the U.N. decision to split British Palestine into separate Jewish and Arab states, a former U.S. Army officer is recruited by the Jews to reorganize the Haganah (Jewish defense force).
- *Gentleman's Agreement.* 1947 drama starring Gregory Peck as a reporter in postwar New York who pretends to be Jewish

to cover a story on antisemitism, and personally discovers the true depths of bigotry and hatred.

- *Golda.* 2023 docudrama starring Helen Mirren as Golda Meir. The focus of the film is Meir's tenure as Prime Minister of Israel during the 1973 Yom Kippur War.
- *Loving Leah.* 2009 romantic drama starring Lauren Ambrose, Adam Kaufman, and Susie Essman. This portrayal of American Jewish culture centers on the love story of a 26-year-old widow and her late husband's brother, a handsome 30-year-old cardiologist.

Documentaries

Arranged in chronological order of the subject matter.

- *The Hope: The Rebirth of Israel.* This 2015 CBN docudrama tells the story of Israel's rebirth through the eyes of the nation's founders, Theodor Herzl, Chaim Weizmann, David Ben-Gurion, and Golda Meir. Available from CBN Films at https://www.cbnfilms.com/thehope.php.
- *Exodus 1947: The Ship that Launched a Nation.* 1997 PBS documentary narrated by Morley Safer. In 1947, as the status of Jewish Holocaust survivors was in limbo, a group of private American citizens bought a steamship to transport 4,500 refugees from France to British Palestine in defiance of British restrictions on Jewish immigration. This is the story of how the resulting international incident was the catalyst for independence of the State of Israel. Available at https://www.exodus1947.com/.
- *In Our Hands: The Battle for Jerusalem.* This 2017 docudrama produced by CBN tells the story of Israel's 55th Paratrooper

Brigade as they fought to liberate their ancestral capital of Jerusalem during the Six Day War. Available from CBN Films at https://www.cbnfilms.com/inourhands.php.

- *Made in Israel.* 2013 CBN documentary explores the roots of Israeli innovation in agriculture, medicine, and technology. Available from CBN Films at https://www.cbnfilms.com/madeinisrael.php.
- *I Am Israel.* This 2017 documentary narrated by John Rhys-Davies is a tour of Israel through the eyes of the Jewish men and women whose very lives are a testimony to the promises of God. Available from The Israel Guys at https://theisraelguys.store/products/i-am-israel.
- *Route 60: The Biblical Highway.* 2024 TBN production with former US Ambassador to Israel David Friedman and former Secretary of State Mike Pompeo. This documentary traces Route 60 through Israel's Biblical Heartland, from Nazareth to Beersheba – the same route travelled by Israel's Patriarchs in ancient times. Available at https://route60.movie/.

News Sources

These sources are a mix of Christian and Jewish (Messianic and non-Messianic), traditional, and alternative media. All have a presence on social media, which at time of this writing includes such popular platforms as Facebook, Instagram, LinkedIn, Rumble, Telegram, TikTok, YouTube, X (formerly Twitter), and WhatsApp.

- Behold Israel (Amir Tsarfati), http://www.beholdisrael.org/
- Berel Solomon, https://www.youtube.com/@BerelSolomon.
- Hananya Naftali, https://www.hnaftali.com/
- Israel Today, https://www.israeltoday.co.il/

- Israel Unwired, https://www.israelunwired.com/
- Israel365 News, https://israel365.com/
- Jewish News Syndicate (JNS), https://www.jns.org/
- Pulse of Israel, https://pulseofisrael.com/
- The Jerusalem Post, https://www.jpost.com/
- The Times of Israel, https://www.timesofisrael.com/
- Yishai Fleisher, https://yishaifleisher.com/
- Christian Broadcasting Network (CBN), https://cbn.com/
- Jerusalem Dateline, https://cbn.com/news/jerusalem-dateline
- TBN Israel, https://www.tbnisrael.com/
- The Israel Guys, https://theisraelguys.com/

Educational Resources

Although some of these sources are intended for Jewish audiences, they are valuable for Christians who want to investigate Jewish viewpoints, especially on biblical studies.

- Aleph Beta, a unique kind of Torah library, featuring original podcasts, short animated videos, deep dive courses, and more. https://alephbeta.org/.
- Center for Jewish-Christian Understanding and Cooperation (CJCUC), a forum for Jewish-Christian relational dialogue. https://www.cjcuc.com/
- Chabad.org, a website dedicated to uniting Jews worldwide, empowering them with knowledge of their 3,300 year-old tradition, and fostering within them a deeper connection to Judaism's rituals and faith. https://www.chabad.org/
- Cry for Zion, a movement of Jews and Christians that supports the Jewish people's rights to sovereignty over Zion—the Temple Mount—guaranteeing Jewish rights and freedoms on

their most holy place. Cry for Zion accomplishes this goal through education and support. https://www.cryforzion.com/

- Friends of Zion (FOZ), a global network of Christians joining together to pray for the peace of Jerusalem. FOZ works through this network to publish peace, bring tidings of love and care to those in need, and demonstrate true Christian love to the Jewish people. https://friendsofzion.com/
- Jewish Virtual Library, a source for information about Jewish history, Israel, U.S.-Israel relations, the Holocaust, antisemitism and Judaism. https://www.jewishvirtuallibrary.org/
- Land of Israel Network, a fellowship that strives to be the authentic Judean voice to the world, sharing the truth, beauty, and divine purpose of Israel. https://thelandofisrael.com/
- March of Life/March of Remembrance, an initiative by Pastors Jobst and Charlotte Bittner from Tübingen, Germany, to organize memorial and reconciliation marches at sites of the Holocaust all over Europe and worldwide. https://marchoflife. org/.
- Root Source, a network that exists to enable, encourage, and enrich relationships between pro-Israel Christians and Jews on a basis of mutual respect and love. The flagship program of Root Source brings knowledgeable, authentic Israeli teachers and inquisitive Christians together to study the Jewish texts foundational to Christian faith. http://root-source.com/
- Sefaria.org, a nonprofit organization dedicated to building the future of Jewish learning in an open and participatory way. Sefaria is assembling a free living library of Jewish texts and their interconnections, in Hebrew and in translation. https:// www.sefaria.org/texts

- Simka Foundation, a ministry that inspires Christian families to grow stronger through the weekly, monthly and seasonal traditions of Jesus, teaching a generation about God's prophetic calendar so they can reclaim the joy of their Hebrew heritage and reduce antisemitism. https://www.simkafoundation.org/
- Ten From the Nations, a nonprofit organization dedicated to spreading awareness and promoting reconciliation between the Christian and Jewish communities. The TFTN mission is to turn the hearts of the Nations toward Jerusalem and the Jewish people through prayer, education, inter-community events, strategic networking, and activism. https://www.tenfromthenations.org/
- The Isaiah Projects, a ministry dedicated to creating and providing specific tools that will help Christians discover the Hebraic roots of their faith. https://www.theisaiahprojects.com/
- The Temple Institute, an organization dedicated to every aspect of the Holy Temple of Jerusalem, and the central role it fulfilled, and will once again fulfill, in the spiritual well-being of both Israel and all the nations of the world. https://templeinstitute.org/
- United States Holocaust Memorial Museum, a living memorial to the Holocaust, inspires citizens and leaders worldwide to confront hatred, prevent genocide, and promote human dignity. Federal support guarantees the Museum's permanent place on the National Mall, and its far-reaching educational programs and global impact are made possible by generous donors. https://www.ushmm.org/
- Yad Vashem: The World Holocaust Remembrance Center, leads the documentation, research, education and commem-

oration of the Holocaust, and conveys the chronicles of this singular Jewish and human event to every person in Israel, to the Jewish people, and to every significant and relevant audience worldwide. https://yadvashem.org/
- ZionismU exists to teach Zionist history, and does so through the Zionism 101 Film Series, Lesson Plans, PowerPoint presentations, supporting documents, and more, much of which is available for free. https://www.zionismu.com/

Israel Advocacy

These sources are more than simply advocacy groups for Israel, the Jewish people, Christian-Jewish relations, and Zionism. Many have a specific purpose, and through that lens provide Israel-related news and commentary.
- Boneh Israel ("Building Israel"): a nonprofit organization focused on building up and reviving important Biblical sites, bringing the Bible to life, educating the nations about the past, present and future of Israel, and actively bringing the redemption closer. This Christian organization has been instrumental in locating the famous Red Heifers for the Temple service. https://www.bonehisrael.com/
- Bridge Connector Ministries: a bridge connecting Christians to Jews, partnering together in our shared goals. https://bridgeconnectorministries.com/
- Christian Friends of Israeli Communities (CFOIC) Heartland was established in 1995, as a Christian response to the Oslo Peace Accords in 1993. CFOIC Heartland provides a much-needed vehicle for Christians to become better informed about the Jewish communities in the heartland of Biblical Israel, to

visit these areas and to provide practical support for vital community needs. https://cfoic.com/

- Christians United for Israel (CUFI), the largest pro-Israel organization in the United States, is the foremost Christian organization educating and empowering millions of Americans to speak and act with one voice in defense of Israel and the Jewish people. https://cufi.org/
- International Christian Embassy Jerusalem (ICEJ) represents Christians around the world who stand with Israel and the Jewish people based on biblical principles and promises. Founded in 1980, the ICEJ recognizes the modern-day restoration of Israel as the faithfulness of God to keep His ancient covenant promises to the Jewish people. https://www.icej.org/
- Israel Allies Foundation (IAF) works to educate and empower pro-Israel, faith-based legislators worldwide. https://israelallies.org/
- Keep God's Land, a grassroots movement dedicated to strengthening and defending Israel's right to its biblical heartland, with the ultimate goal of Israeli sovereignty over Judea and Samaria. https://keepgodsland.com/
- One Jewish State, a movement created by former U.S. Ambassador David Friedman dedicated to establishing Israeli sovereignty over its Biblical homeland, ensuring freedom and prosperity for all inhabitants, and achieving peace between Israelis and Palestinians. https://www.onejewishstate.net/
- Proclaiming Justice to the Nations (PJTN), a nonprofit organization that educates, advocates, and moves to activate Christians, Jews and all people of conscience in building a global community of action and prayer in support of Israel and the Jewish people. https://pjtn.org/

- Regavim is a public movement dedicated to the protection of Israel's national lands and resources. Regavim acts to prevent illegal seizure of state land, and to protect the rule of law and clean government in matters pertaining to land-use policy in the State of Israel. https://www.regavim.org/
- Stand With Us is an international, non-partisan education organization that supports Israel and fights antisemitism. https://www.standwithus.com/

Israel-Focused Ministries and Charities

- Aliyah Return Center (ARC), is an Israel based registered nonprofit organization, helping new Jewish immigrants establish roots in the land of Israel and thrive. https://aliyahreturncenter.com/
- Altar of Prayer (AOP), a 24/7 Global Prayer for Aliyah (Jewish return to Israel). AOP is an intercessory ministry with a prophetic task to assist participants in understanding God's purposes for Israel, enabling them to pray effectively. https://www.altarofprayer.com/
- Christian Friends of Israel (CFI) – Jerusalem exists to comfort and to support the people of Israel, and to inform Christians around the world of God's plans for Israel. https://www.cfijerusalem.org/
- Genesis 123 Foundation is a US based nonprofit whose mission is to build bridges between Jews and Christians with Israel in ways that are new, unique, and meaningful. https://genesis123.co/
- Greening Israel Project seeks to reverse the damage done to Israel's land and ecosystem by foreign nations over the centu-

ries by planting trees as part of the restoration that was prophesied about in the Bible. https://greeningisrael.com/

- HaYovel brings believers from all over the world to serve the land and people of Israel by planting trees, harvesting grapes, pruning vines, and much more. https://serveisrael.com/
- Return Ministries has a vision of Jews and Christians working together to fulfill God's plans and purposes for Israel and the nations according to the Word of God. This is accomplished by assisting Christians to return to their Judeo/Christian roots so as to fulfill our God-ordained destiny and assisting the Jewish people to return and be restored to their God-given inheritance in Israel, all in preparation for the return of the Jewish Messiah. https://www.return.co.il/
- Shalom Jerusalem Foundation, founded by Rabbi Yehuda Glick, embraces the mission to redeem the Temple Mount and ensure all religions enjoy total freedom of access to and worship on the Mount, in order to turn the Mount into the prophetic House of Prayer for All Nations and pave the road for the rebuilding of the Third Temple. https://www.shalomjerusalem.org/
- Shiloh Israel Childrens Fund was created to enable healing and the easing of trauma from terrorism in children, so that they can grow into adulthood with a brighter future. The vision of the Shiloh Israel Children's Fund is to enable generations of children not to be victims. Our deepest trauma can either define us or refine us into who we are supposed to be. https://www.israelchildren.org/
- Succat Hallel (Hebrew for Tent of Praise), is a dynamic community of worshippers and intercessors from five continents

drawn together to stand as watchmen on the walls of Jerusalem. https://succathallel.com/

- The Return Israel is an outgrowth of the national and global day of prayer and repentance called The Return that took place in Washington, DC, on September 26, 2020. The Return works toward revival by individual, national, and global repentance. A big part of that is reconciliation between Jews and Gentiles, blessing the land and people of Israel, and praying together for the peace of Jerusalem. https://thereturn.org/israel/

- Vision for Israel (VFI) is a nonprofit charitable organization that has provided humanitarian aid, disaster relief, and community support for over 26 years. VFI is committed to decreasing poverty in Israel—and spreading love, truth, and healing to the people who need it the most. https://www.visionforisrael.com/en

- Emunah (Hebrew for Faith) in Israel provides life-changing services to help the most vulnerable children and families to break the cycle of distress, and to build their own rewarding and stable lives and families. World Emunah serves as the liaison and umbrella organization for all the dynamic Emunah affiliates in many countries throughout the world who raise vital funds to support Emunah's work in Israel. https://www.worldemunah.org/

- Yad Leah (Hebrew for Hand of Leah) is an American-based Jewish nonprofit that provides quality clothing to thousands of needy families across Israel—empowering them with confidence, dignity, and self-respect. https://yadleah.org/

Israeli Products, Tours, and Business Opportunities

- Blessed Buy Israel, online store offering a range of products from Judea and Samaria. https://blessedbuyisrael.com/
- Lev HaOlam, subscription service for a monthly box of products from Judea and Samaria. https://tl.levhaolam.com/
- Jerusalem Tours International (JTI), specializing in Pilgrimages and Leisure travel to the Holy Land (Israel), Jordan, Egypt and Europe. https://jerusalemtours.com/
- Keshet Educational Journeys explores Israel as a tapestry of significant ideas in Jewish and Christian history which has impacted all of humanity. The goal is to experience and understand Israel on its many levels and in all its complexities. https://www.keshetisrael.co.il/
- Kol Yehuda: A Voice from Judah is tour guide Hanoch Young. His goal is to help everyone have the kind of Israel experience that will change their lives. https://www.kolyehuda.com/
- Lipkin Tours, offers customized tours to bring groups that wish to become identified with Israel and the Jewish people, with a strong emphasis on visiting the regions of Judea and Samaria. https://www.lipkintours.com/
- Hillel Fuld, Israel's top marketer, with leading tech entrepreneurs, investors, and visionaries to accompany them on their journey from idea to revenue. https://www.hillelfuld.com/
- Startup Nation Central, an independent nonprofit organization that gives global solution seekers an 'All Access Pass' to Israel's bold and determined innovators, to their expertise, and to the solutions they offer. https://startupnationcentral.org/

ABOUT THE AUTHOR

Albert J. McCarn grew up in the Evangelical environment of a Southern Baptist church, a Presbyterian Christian school, and a curiosity about Pentecostal aspects of the faith. What he learned in his formative years was that the doctrinal differences of these streams of Christianity were actually different perspectives on the same scriptural truth, and therefore should not be causes of division among those who profess to be disciples of Jesus Christ. That lesson of seeking common ground rather than division informed his future encounters with Christians of other streams (Anglican, Catholic, Orthodox), Jews (Messianic and Orthodox), Muslims, and people of no particular faith.

Al's biblical worldview was refined in his academic endeavors, including an undergraduate degree in Russian and German from Florida State University, masters degrees in International Relations from the University of Southern California and History from the University of Alabama-Birmingham, and half a PhD (he never finished his dissertation) in History at the University of Arizona.

His studies emphasized Western encounters with Islam. That mirrored his professional experience as a US Army Intelligence officer, specializing in counterintelligence and counter-terrorism, especially Islamist terrorism. Al encountered terrorism at the beginning of his career of nearly 30 years when, on the eve of his first tour of duty in Germany, Hezbollah terrorists murdered 220 Marines and 18 Sailors in a bombing attack on their barracks in Beirut. His professional experience over the decades shaped his understanding of the Israeli-Arab conflict, and the wider conflicts in the Middle East as the US became actively involved in lengthy wars in Iraq and Afghanistan.

Even before retiring from the Army in 2012, Al knew he was to be part of the bridge God is building between Christians and Jews. With that in mind, he became part of the facilitation team of Prayer Surge Now in 2009, a ministry that connects intercessors through weekly conference calls. In 2016, Al partnered with fellow followers of Jesus to establish B'ney Yosef North America, a ministry of reconciliation that emphasizes the Hebraic nature of the Christian faith. In 2019, at the encouragement of Bob O'Dell, he became part of the prayer and planning team for Nations' 9th of Av (now called Ten From the Nations), a ministry dedicated to educating Christians about our history with the Jewish people and healing the breach between us. That has led to other connections, which is how Al became part of the Advisory Board for Root Source and an advocate for Zionism.

Al and his wife, Charlayne, make their home in South Carolina, where they are active members of Founded in Truth Fellowship.